# The
# ESSENTIAL
# 55

D1009914

## RON CLARK

# *The*
# ESSENTIAL
# 55

## AN AWARD-WINNING EDUCATOR'S RULES FOR DISCOVERING THE SUCCESSFUL STUDENT IN EVERY CHILD

••••••••••••••••••••••••••••••

*Revised and Updated Edition*

••••••••••••••••••••••••••••••

# RON CLARK

hachette
BOOKS

NEW YORK   BOSTON

Hachette Books
Hachette Book Group
1290 Avenue of the Americas
New York, NY 10104
hachettebookgroup.com
twitter.com/hachettebooks

Originally published in hardcover by Hyperion Books in April 2003; originally published in ebook by Hyperion Books in September 2003; originally published in paperback by Hyperion Books in August 2004

First edition: May 2003

First Revised Edition: April 2019

Hachette Books is a division of Hachette Book Group, Inc.

The Hachette Books name and logo are trademarks of Hachette Book Group, Inc.

The publisher is not responsible for websites (or their content) that are not owned by the publisher.

The Hachette Speakers Bureau provides a wide range of authors for speaking events. To find out more, go to www.hachettespeakersbureau.com or call (866) 376-6591.

Library of Congress Control Number: 2019930068

ISBNs: 978-0-316-42477-6 (revised paperback), 978-1-4013-0001-2 (ancillary edition hardcover); 978-1-4013-9858-3 (ebook)

Printed in the United States of America

LSC-H

Printing 5, 2021

# CONTENTS

TO MOM AND DAD
*Thank you for letting me stand on your shoulders.*

AND

TO MY STUDENTS
*Thank you for teaching me more about life than
I could ever teach you.*

# INTRODUCTION

This small, humble book you are holding built a miraculous dream.

I was teaching in Harlem when I had the honor of being named as Disney's "Teacher of the Year." I was twenty-nine years old and weighed 140 pounds. I was running on pure adrenaline and a desire to help the children I taught.

I was asked to appear on *The Oprah Winfrey Show*, and I showed up in an oversized shirt and an old tie. The ladies in the green room said, "If we had more time we would cut that hair and make it more presentable." I obviously had no idea how that day would change my life completely.

During the interview, Ms. Winfrey mentioned that she thought I should write a book, and, well, when Oprah Winfrey tells you to write a book, you write a book.

The book you now hold is the culmination of that recommendation. I took Ms. Winfrey's advice and placed the methods I use for helping my students within these pages. When the book was published, Ms. Winfrey asked me to appear on her show so she could profile it. This time, the hair was on point—or at least I thought it was at the time. I spiked it with handfuls of mousse and held a blow dryer to it for three minutes. When I look back on the footage of the interview, I wonder, *Ron, what were you thinking?*

During the interview, Ms. Winfrey shouted, "I love this book! I love your rules!" She encouraged everyone watching to go out and buy a copy, and one hour after the show, the book was the number two book in the nation, right behind *Harry Potter*. It stayed there for four months, and all proceeds were placed in a foundation and used to build a dream: a school like no other in the world!

I was intent on building a school filled with exuberant children who were thrilled about learning, innovative teachers who were excited to be there, and a passionate flair for creative approaches. I wanted the school to be at the forefront of innovation in our country, and I hoped it would spark a revolution.

If you ask fifth graders what they want to be when they grow up, they don't say "teacher" anymore. And if they do say "teacher," people say, "But you're so smart, there are so many things you could do." Teacher pay is low, discipline is getting worse, and parents can be difficult. Children see this and they aren't jumping to say, "I want to be in that profession when I grow up!" I hoped to build a school that would show people that education can be young, fun, exhilarating, challenging, and powerful. The idea was to join together the best teachers in the world to work at the school, and invite educators to come and witness our methods in person. At the time, I hoped we might host up to sixty teachers per week. I soon realized my expectations were far too low.

Currently, the Ron Clark Academy (RCA) has 600 educators visit our school each week to learn about our methods and strategies, which they then take back to implement in their various school systems. It's like Disneyland for educators, and tens of thousands have visited. There are countless stories of the revolution we started and how it has affected millions of children around our country as well as globally. It is mind blowing!

One of the key aspects of each educator's visit to RCA is that they learn The Essential 55, the system of rules listed within this book. It is the bedrock of our school, and it has allowed us to have the structure necessary to be truly innovative and bring vibrant lessons to life. This book contains the keys to my success as a teacher and the strategies that have proven effective when working with even the most challenging of children. Over the years, these rules have evolved and changed in many beautiful and useful ways. It is for this reason that I decided to revise this book: to showcase some new rules and how older rules have evolved. These rules have been around the world and impacted children from China to Italy and Finland to Australia. I am honored to now share them with you.

Ron Clark

April 2019

# THE BEGINNING

Her name was Mudder. She loved *Guiding Light*, collards, and snuff, and she was my grandmother. Mudder stood right at five feet, but when she placed her hands on her hips, she was the tallest person in the room. She was definitely a lady who didn't put up with any nonsense, and she was respected by everyone around her; poor be the person who had to learn that the hard way. As I grew up, she lived with my family and had a strong impact on who I am today. She's one of the reasons I feel so strongly about these fifty-five expectations I have of my students, as well as all people. She, along with my parents, gave me a true southern upbringing, which included respect, manners, and an appreciation of others. In addition to those ideals, I was shown how to enjoy life, take advantage of opportunities, and live every moment to the fullest. I was very fortunate to be surrounded by family members who were excellent examples of how life should be lived and not taken for granted.

Once I became a teacher, it became evident to me that many children aren't exposed to the type of guidance and opportunities that I had when I was growing up. I have tried to set an example for my students and be a role model like my family members were for me. Over the years of working with kids and watching this list grow from five rules to a handbook of life's lessons, I have seen a remarkable difference in the way my students hold themselves, perform in school, and have respect for others.

I use these lessons with much success with my students, but they are not only for children; most of the fifty-five items can apply to anyone, young and old, from the housewife to the doctor, the politician to the waiter, and everyone in between. These lessons are about how we live, interact with others, and appreciate life, and, therefore, they speak to everyone.

I feel so fortunate to have had the opportunity to work with children firsthand and develop the list of fifty-five rules into what it is today. It is an extension of my upbringing mixed with lessons I have learned about life, along with some rules that I felt the need to adopt to maintain order with my students and get them to achieve their potential. However, the rules are more than about getting kids to behave; they're about preparing kids for what awaits them after they leave my classroom. It is about preparing them to handle any situation they encounter and give them the confidence to do so. In some ways, it is a fifty-five-step plan. The steps, however, are not sequential; they are all explained, practiced, and enforced from day one in the classroom. At the end of the year, I like to say that my students are "polished." I know I can take them anywhere, put them in any situation, and present them with any lesson, because they are at a point where they are receptive to learning and eager to experience life.

Throughout college, I found that my one true love in life was adventure. I was up for any type of challenge that came my way, and that certainly led me to my share of wild moments. I once ran across the field of a nationally televised football game with my friend Bri, wearing only boxers and painted purple from head to toe, as we were chased by a gaggle of police officers in hot pursuit. While working at Dunkin' Donuts, and during a game of hide-and-seek, I hid in a warm, locked oven that was turned on. Because I had accidentally locked my coworker out of the building, I was almost cooked to death. Even though I am terrified of heights, I have bungee jumped, climbed mountains, rappelled off cliffs, and parasailed behind a boat off the Atlantic coast. When I graduated from college, I realized I definitely did not want to teach. Actually, I didn't want to work at all. In search of more adventures, I moved to London and worked as a singing and dancing waiter. After six months of using my southern accent as a British tourist attraction, I left England and backpacked across Europe. I finally ending up in Romania, where I stayed with a family who fed me rat, which made me so sick that I had to be flown home. My adventures certainly had their share of highs and lows, but even when I ended up sick, almost cooked or in trouble with the law, the experiences were worth the costs, because I always walked away a stronger, wiser, and better person.

After I arrived home from Romania, my parents were extremely happy to see me, but I had no intention of remaining home for long. My mother, however, was willing to do whatever it took to get me to stay put. She told me of a fifth-grade teacher in our area who had recently passed away. It was a sudden illness, and her students, the faculty, and the entire community were affected by her loss. Now let me tell you, we live in the country, and the population of Aurora is about 600. You have to drive twenty minutes to get to a stoplight, and it is difficult to entice teachers to the school because of the travel it would require each day. Mom told me that substitute teachers had taken over the teaching position for a month, and that the class had become very unruly. The school was about seventy-five percent minority and most of the kids were on free or reduced-price lunch. I felt sorry for the students, but I was not interested in taking over this class of demanding, high-energy fifth graders, many of whom had behavior problems and learning disabilities.

I told my mother there was no way in this world that I was going to teach at that school, and that I intended to fly to China and run down the Great Wall before then moving to the beaches of California. When she told me I had no money to do such things, I responded that I intended to earn the money while working at Dunkin' Donuts. The next day, I was the first person to arrive at Snowden Elementary School.

Even though I agreed to meet with the principal, I had no intention of taking the job. My Aunt Carolyn worked there as a secretary, so I figured it would give me the opportunity to see her before flying off to California. Upon arrival, I visited with my aunt, and then the principal, Andrea Roberson, gave me a tour of the school and told me about the group of students

I would teach if I accepted the position. She told me about how demanding the students were, of several with learning disabilities, and how I had to raise those test scores no matter what. I remember thinking to myself, "And this lady is actually trying to convince me to work here." I did act interested, but my heart wasn't in it. She then escorted me to the room that held the fifth-grade class. We walked in and there was a little boy named Rayquan sitting just a few feet from the door. He looked up at me with his huge, brown, round eyes and said, "Is you gonna be our new teacher?" I can't explain the feeling that came over me; it was like an epiphany. The instant trust in his voice, the excitement all over his face, and his evident longing for stability called out to me. I knew that was where I was supposed to be. I looked back at Rayquan and said, "I think so."

Before taking over the class myself, the principal wanted me to observe the substitute teacher. She didn't want to just throw me in the class with no idea about what to expect from the group. The substitute in question, Mrs. Waddle, was an eccentric lady who always had a sandwich in one hand and whose matted wigs always seemed to lean to one side. On the first day I observed her, she became upset with a student who didn't know the answer to a question. She proceeded to draw three small circles in a row on the blackboard. She then instructed the young man to place his nose in the middle circle and one finger from each hand in the outside circles. She left him there and turned back to the class and asked the question again. The next student got the question right, and she threw her hands in the air and proclaimed that she felt the Holy Spirit. She then sang an entire verse of "Amazing

Grace." Sitting there and watching this teacher for a week solidified more and more each day my desire to work with those students. They needed me more than I could have ever imagined. Before turning the class over to me, Mrs. Waddle left me with one bit of "wisdom." She looked at me and said, "You know, Mr. Clark, you'll do fine. As long as you can affect the life of one child, you've been a success."

To this day, I do not like that quote. I feel we have to approach education with the determination to affect each and every one of our students. The mentality of achieving "success" after reaching one child isn't enough. I approach each year with the knowledge that I have only one year to make a life's worth of difference in each child in that classroom, and I give it everything I've got. I didn't know much when I first entered the classroom and took over that class from Mrs. Waddle, but I did know my life was going to be different, because I was determined to give my students a different life, a better life. My time as a teacher had begun.

During my time in the classroom, my experiences were like a roller-coaster ride, with invitations to the White House, 911 calls, trips around the country with students, projects that garnered worldwide attention, and a major move from teaching in rural North Carolina to Harlem in New York City. Those events highlight my time spent working with children and my efforts to teach them these fifty-five rules. I recount many of the stories here. They show the highs and lows, successes and disappointments, and lessons learned along the way.

As you go through the list, there are some rules you may like and use with students and children in your life, and there may be some that don't inspire you. We all have different levels of tolerance when it comes to the behavior of children, and we all have different levels of expectations for ourselves and others. I offer these rules as suggestions, as tried-and-true methods that have served my students well. I hope you find them useful.

## RULE 1

*Be humble.*

I think it is important to lead with this rule. In life, as long as you make decisions and start from a place where you try to shine more light on others than on yourself, you are living right. When you choose to highlight the gifts and talents of others, they will, in turn, be more likely to point out your accomplishments.

It's getting harder to nurture this lesson in my students. On social media, they see so many people trying to get attention with countless selfies and posts about their accomplishments. We were on a trip to Washington, D.C. with our fifth graders and I took a picture of students in front of the Capitol. A few minutes later, one of the children asked, "Mr. Clark, how many likes has it gotten so far?" As the trip went on, I realized a few of the students were more concerned with getting in pictures and being on social media than enjoying the trip itself. These kids are the product of a changing society where they live through the perception of others.

When we first opened Ron Clark Academy, I introduced one of our students, Kennedy, to a donor. I said, "Kennedy is the MVP of our basketball team." The donor looked at

Kennedy and said, "Wow, you must really be good," and she replied, "Yes ma'am." Later, after the donor left, I told Kennedy that it's okay for her to be aware that she is the best player, but when someone points it out, she should be humble and praise others. When the donor said, "Wow, you must really be good," I told Kennedy she should have responded by saying, "I am blessed to be on a team with a lot of really hardworking players," or "I'm lucky to have a coach that really believes in our team. She inspires us all to be our best."

At RCA, it's a great honor to be valedictorian, and that student receives a lot of attention. When people congratulate them, I encourage them to respond with comments such as, "The entire class is filled with students who spent the last four years working very hard, and I think we all encouraged each other to try our absolute best," or "My parents really encouraged me to work hard over the past four years, and it's because of their support that I was able to stay focused and achieve my goals." I tell my students that if they are on a team and a teammate says to them, "You killed it today," they should respond by saying, "I always play well when you are on my team," or "It was easy to make shots when you were giving me such incredible passes."

There are times, however, when students are too humble. When I taught in North Carolina, we had students who went for scholarship interviews. They were very qualified, but they didn't receive the scholarships. It baffled me! I arranged a mock interview to see what was going on. When I asked one student, "What are some of your favorite hobbies?" he would respond with one-word answers like, "Robotics." I recall exclaiming, "But you just won first place in the regional competition. Why not mention that?" The student said he didn't want to brag.

Sometimes it's necessary to shine some light on yourself: when you are in a job interview, filling out a scholarship application or trying to get people to see the worth in your opinion. When I talk to groups of educators, I want them to know that I have traveled widely to learn about our education system. If I say it the wrong way, it will come across as boasting. So I say, "I feel so fortunate to have had the opportunity to travel to all fifty states to learn more about our nation's education system." I encouraged the young robotics student to respond to a question about his hobbies by saying, "My favorite hobby is robotics! My team and I have been preparing for the regional competition for the last six months. We met every Saturday and worked extremely hard to prepare our robot for whatever challenges would be presented. Just this past weekend, we had the honor of winning first place. It was an amazing feeling to be part of such a focused and dedicated team. I learned a lot about preparation, problem solving, and how to set a goal and accomplish it."

The key point I want my students to understand is you should take a moment where people praise you and turn it into a moment where you seek to praise others. When you accept a compliment as if you deserve to receive the praise, then you will be seen as arrogant and egotistical, and it will diminish your skills and abilities in the eyes of others. When you make an effort to include others in an accomplishment, not only will they recognize your talent, they will also see you as gracious, humble, and a true team player.

# RULE 2

*Make eye contact. When someone is speaking, keep your eyes on him or her at all times. If someone makes a comment, turn and face that person.*

Keeping eye contact is something that many people find hard to do, but it is important when you are trying to get your point across to people and show them you are serious about what you are saying. For example, if you talk to your boss and ask for a raise, you are far more likely to be taken seriously if you look the boss in the eyes rather than glance downward. If you make a business proposal, people will be more likely to trust you and believe in your ideas if they see that you are confident, sure of yourself, and make eye contact with them.

I spend a lot of time encouraging my students to practice this skill. To give them practice, I put the kids in groups of two. I then tell them that making eye contact when you make a statement gives what you say more emphasis and emotion. When you look away or down at the floor, it shows you aren't sure of what you are saying and that you possibly aren't telling the truth. I also tell them that I have heard that repeated glances to the upper left-hand side mean you are being dishonest. Once they are in their groups, I have them practice talking to each other, taking note of how effective they are at maintaining eye contact with their partners.

Making eye contact is not only a way to show confidence, but it is also an important way to show respect. In class, when a student expresses an opinion, I make sure all of the other students turn and focus on that individual. I don't allow them to raise their hands to make additional comments until that person is finished because, if they do, it looks as if they are more concerned with what they want to say than with the opinions of the speaker. I tell them to imagine what it would be like if they were trying to express a thought and everyone around them kept waving their hands. It would make them feel like their opinions had no value, and so, therefore, we don't do it.

I can remember when I was in school that it was awfully hard to daydream while staring at the teacher. If I could focus on the head in front of me or on my pencil, I was good to go, but watching the teacher just took something out of it. Therefore, I make sure to have all eyes on me at all times. That way, as I teach, I can see the looks on the students' faces and can tell if they are confused and lost or engaged and attentive. Also, since I am a very visual learner and teacher, I constantly make motions with my hands and on the board, and I want the kids to follow along with me and know exactly where I'm coming from.

I have worked many a day in fast food. I've spent countless hours making the doughnuts at Dunkin' Donuts and waiting tables at various restaurants. Serving the public can be a thrill, but it can also be torture when you have to deal with difficult customers. I always liked it when people would look me in the eye to give their order. It is far more respectful to look a person full in the face. As they were leaving, I always expected them to say thank you, but many didn't, and it baffled me. What were they thinking? Many who did say thank you just said it as they turned away or drove off. Why not take one second to look the person in the eyes and say thank you as if you mean it?

I try to get my students to practice doing this with various adults in the school who aren't teachers. Often custodians, cafeteria workers, secretaries, and teachers' aides aren't considered worthy of the respect teachers get, and I work hard to change that image in the minds of my students. I explain to the students the role of each person at the school and why their job makes it possible for kids to get a great education. I then tell them that people work harder and with more effort if they feel they are appreciated and that they are making a difference. I make sure I model the type of behavior I expect as I interact with all members of the staff in a friendly and respectful manner. It doesn't take much effort before the students are following my lead, and the results are always obvious. When we go to the lunchroom, the students aren't allowed to talk in the line, and when they get their food, they must look the cafeteria workers in the eyes and say, "May I," when asking for anything. In turn, they always thank the lunchroom workers and tell them to have a good day. The workers always comment on how wonderful the class is and how much they appreciate the respect.

No matter how we interact with others around us and regardless of what we say, we are taken more seriously and our actions are much more appreciated if they come with eye contact.

# RULE 3

*Seek to uplift others. If someone in the class wins a game or does something well, we congratulate that person. Claps should be of at least three seconds in length with the full part of both hands meeting in a manner that will give the appropriate clap volume. (I know stating it that way makes me sound like a nut, but it's important to spell it out.)*

Think about a football or basketball game. What happens when someone scores a touchdown or makes a winning basket? The crowd goes crazy and cheers for that person. I think we should have that type of supportive environment and camaraderie in all areas where we have to work together to achieve goals, whether it be the workplace, the home or especially the classroom. Any time people are given praise and rewarded for their efforts, they are going to do a better job.

In life, I have learned that when you are at your lowest, one of the best ways to pull yourself up is to seek to uplift others. I tell my students that if your intention is to always uplift those around you that they will, in turn, lift you up. If your intention is to pull others down so that you can raise yourself, then others will drag you down with them.

I give the class examples of times when it would be appropriate to clap for other students. Sometimes it may happen after a good comment, a high test score, or an exceptional piece of writing. Also, if someone has a low score, we should still clap if that score shows improvement. We then go through a few role-playing exercises and practice clapping—yes, practice clapping. There can be no halfway clapping, as I call it. All of the students must clap in a way that shows respect and appreciation. Before I began to teach students how to clap, I would have half of the class clapping, a quarter of the class barely touching hands, and the rest of the class on some distant planet. After some detailed instruction, they were all on board.

Sometimes students start to clap for someone's comment or score that might not necessarily deserve applause. The rule is, if a few students start to clap, we all start to clap. Apparently, those who started to clap saw something they appreciated. It is far worse to have only a few weak claps than for us all to clap for something that might not be worthy.

As one teacher in a classroom with thirty-seven students, it was near impossible to give all of the students the attention and praise they deserved. It made it a lot easier when I had a classroom of students who were constantly looking to applaud each other's achievements. Acknowledgment from the teacher is always appreciated, but praise from a student's peers can have a much greater impact.

Teachers who visit my classroom always comment on how I have my students' grades posted around the room. This seems a bit unorthodox, because teachers are usually told to keep grades confidential in order to spare students' feelings. I find that sharing the grades with the entire class can be a very positive experience in the right type of environment. First of all, I don't post all grades—that would be impossible. I try to pick grades for assignments that all students, with effort, can do well on, because you don't want to embarrass a child who struggles for any reason. Second, I try to pick assignments and grades that can be tracked over a period of time. For example, each night the students are given a reading assignment. The following morning, they are given a multiple-choice test that I read aloud, based on the assignment. I can grade the tests in less than five minutes, and I always have them ready to hand back on the same day. As I hand them back, I write the scores on a chart that remains posted for the entire grading period. When I list the scores, I make a huge production out of it. I call the student's name, pause for a couple of seconds, and then I shout out the score—if it is 100, at the top of my lungs. The class cheers and the student's face lights up like crazy. A score of ninety also receives claps and an eighty and some-times even a seventy receives claps if a student has shown improvement. The students love this, and they look forward to it all day.

One of the people who I have met who best illustrates how to uplift others is Korey Collins. He was visiting one of our teacher training experiences at RCA, and at the end of the first day when the 600 visiting educators left to go back to their hotels, I asked our staff to help me set up the chairs in the gymnasium for the next morning's breakfast. As we were working, I noticed that Korey was helping us stack chairs. I ran over to him and said, "Sir, you should head on to the hotel. We've got this." Korey responded, "Oh, I'm already here. It's what I do. Do you mind if I stay and help?" I said okay, and for about an hour he helped us move chairs and clean the gym. Before we left, I asked my staff to be at RCA at six in the morning to prepare for the visiting educators who would arrive back at 8:15 A.M.

At 6 A.M. my staff and I were setting up tables and Korey walked in. I called to him and said, "Sir, you aren't supposed to be here until 8:15 A.M.," and he replied, "Oh, I know, but I heard you say you needed help for 6 A.M. I'm already here; do you mind if I stay and help? It's what I do." Instantly I realized what was going on: he wanted a job. All of his actions were to look good in our eyes so that he would have a leg up when applying to teach with us. After all, RCA is like Hogwarts and Disneyland for teachers. It's an amazing place, and I couldn't blame him. I even decided to give him the benefit of the doubt, and I found him at lunch in order to have a conversation with him. As I cut my turkey, I said, "So, I assume that you've probably applied to teach at our school." To that he replied, "No way, there is no way I would want to work here." My heart sank. "Huh," I replied. He continued, "Man, I have five kids and they are all under the age of seven. My wife and I live in a small community in Pennsylvania and we would never leave there."

It was then that I asked if I could contact his principal to tell him that he impressed me. Korey seemed to think that was odd but he agreed.

The moment the principal picked up the phone, he said, "Who is this? Ron Clark? Why are you calling me? You will NOT talk to Korey Collins and you will NOT offer him a job. He's the best we've got in the whole district." My eyebrows rose. "Really? Tell me more."

I hired Korey Collins. If you are a good administrator, you learn to recruit, and I knew I had to have Korey on my team. I flew his wife and those five kids to Atlanta for the interview.

I'm not even good with babies but I was burping kids and offering to change diapers.

Korey is one of the most important members of our team, and one of the main reasons for it is that he seeks to uplift others at every chance he gets. He cheers for students, colleagues, and parents. He wants to see others do well, and he has no ego or jealousy within him. He's simply an incredible person. The reason I knew he would be like that was because of the way he offered to help with the chairs. He wanted nothing from it; he just genuinely sought to help, to contribute and to uplift the cause.

I make every effort to add people like Korey to RCA's staff, not only because they are incredible members of the team, but because they serve as outstanding role models for our students. Every chance I get, I point out to my students the actions of staff members like Korey that go above and beyond. I want them to notice when Mr. Walker offers to run to Walmart to pick up extra supplies, or when Dr. Jones takes the time to pick up trash off the floor in the cafeteria. I want them to observe how Mr. Bernardin is always high-fiving other members of the staff and how Mr. Thompson never, ever complains. I point these things out to the students so they will start to see that those qualities are ones that should be admired and embodied. I want my students to realize that when you make every effort to contribute to the greater whole and uplift those around you that not only will it be noticed but it will be applauded and commended.

## RULE 4

*During discussions, respect other students' comments, opinions, and ideas. When possible, make statements like, "I agree with John, and I also feel that…" or, "I disagree with Sara. She made a good point, but I feel that…" or, "I think Victor made an excellent observation, and it made me realize…"*

This is a rule I feel should be imposed in every boardroom and meeting in every workplace in America, as well as at every family dinner table. Too often we disregard the comments of others and don't set the type of climate that allows people to speak freely and voice their thoughts and opinions. All too often, people are worried about what others will think of their ideas, and that they will be ridiculed or belittled. I imagine there are hundreds of times every day when the best idea in the room goes unheard or isn't even voiced.

I do not want that type of environment in my classroom, so I developed a system with my kids that creates a supportive and nonthreatening atmosphere. I want to have more than just a class where students are allowed to give their opinions; I want those thoughts and ideas to develop into a discussion with a mutual appreciation for all opinions. For this to happen, I find it necessary to teach the students, step-by-step, how to tell each other that they agree or disagree with the other's comments in a respectful and supportive way.

The first thing I tell my students is that we will never

laugh or make fun of someone's comments. Every person in the class has something to contribute, and in order for our class to be the best it can be, we need to hear the opinions and ideas of everyone. I tell them it is okay to disagree, and it is only human to not agree with everyone about everything. I point out, though, that there is a correct way and an incorrect way to let your feelings be known. We are each different, with different gifts, different experiences, and different roads that we have been down. There is no way to know all of the things that make up your neighbor's ideas. Therefore, we should just appreciate others' statements without being condescending or making them feel their way of thinking isn't right.

We practice this a great deal; for many students, it is as if they are listening to one another's statements and taking value in what other people are saying for the first time. I can tell my students over and over how much I appreciate something they have said or that they made a very smart comment, but when a peer turns and says, "Wow, that was a great idea. I didn't think of that," it is valuable beyond words for that child's self-esteem and confidence. It is very similar to how it is wonderful to hear praise from our mothers, but it can mean more to us when those positive comments and acceptance come from our coworkers.

After a few months in Harlem, I began to see a difference in the students I was teaching, and it was evident to others as well. Individuals who visited our school and observed my class always commented on how polite and supportive the students were of one another. They were amazed by how the students thoroughly enjoyed discussing ideas and how there was a mutual appreciation for all comments and opinions. I noticed the change firsthand in several ways. When I first started teaching in Harlem, I tried to get the students to teach me how to jump rope double Dutch-style. They weren't very supportive at first, and when I made an attempt to jump the ropes, I didn't get any advice or extra tries. They let me have just two attempts and then I had to go to the back of the line.

I noticed that if you were good at jumping rope, all of the other students respected you; it was a major status symbol, and I knew that if I could do it, I would win points with the kids. I tried over and over, but every day they just laughed at me. It seemed as if they didn't even want to give me the chance because they knew it would take too much time and I would never be able to do it anyway. Nevertheless, I was out there each day, trying it over and over. Oftentimes the ropes hit me in the face and I looked awkward jumping all around trying to do it. The kids used to say that when I tried to double Dutch I looked like a horse jumping up and down. Finally, after a few weeks, I started to notice a change in the kids. They started not only to become more supportive of one another in the classroom, but they became more compassionate and caring outside the classroom as well. After three weeks of trying, I was just about to give up on ever being able to jump rope. One of the ropes actually slapped me on the forehead and gave me a pretty bad scratch. Mr. Clark's days of trying to jump rope were over; but then the kids surrounded me and told me they believed in me and that I could do it. They turned the ropes slowly and talked me through it, giving advice and cheering me on. One girl said, "First, Mr. Clark, you've got to stop jumping like a horse. Jump like this." Every child wanted to show me his or her own technique, and it became obvious that they cared about my succeeding. Soon, I went to jump in, expecting the usual slap in the face with the ropes, but something happened. I got in! I was actually jumping successfully between the ropes, and once I got in, I was in for good! I jumped for about thirty seconds straight screaming at the top of my lungs, "I'm in! I'm in!" All of the kids around the playground ran over to see, and they started cheering, "Go Mr. Clark! Go Mr. Clark!" The kids were as thrilled as I was and our relationship improved dramatically after that.

Often in class when I tried to teach difficult subject matter and the kids felt they couldn't do it, I'd say, "Now listen to me! You know...I didn't think I could double Dutch, but you believed in me and you supported me, and I did it. Now, you don't think you can do this work, but I believe in you and I am here to show you I have faith in your ability, and know you will succeed." That really opened the kids' eyes. They often told people, "Mr. Clark supports us when we need him, and we support him when he needs us, because he does need us sometimes and we teach him things, too." Creating the type of environment where everyone supports each other and shows appreciation for the thoughts and abilities of others makes a world of difference in a classroom or in any other group of people who are trying to work together.

# RULE 5

*If you win or do well at something, do not brag. If you lose, do not show anger. Instead, say something like, "I really enjoyed the competition, and I look forward to playing you again," or, "Good game," or don't say anything at all. To show anger or sarcasm, such as "I wasn't playing hard anyway. You really aren't that good," shows weakness.*

If you are good at something, others will recognize it. There is no need to tell others how talented you are, because by bragging about yourself, you are seen in a negative light, and people won't care about what skills you may have. This is obviously hard for many people to realize, because we seem to live in a culture where everyone wants to put their accomplishments and abilities on display. I used to be a huge fan of one certain movie/TV star/rapper. I thought he was extremely talented, and I enjoyed his work very much.

As of late, however, every time I see him on TV or read about him in magazines he is very cocky and makes statements to the effect that he is the greatest performer alive. It has really disappointed me so much and made me avoid paying to see anything that he is involved with. The shame is, everyone knows he is talented; there is no need for him to toot his own horn.

I don't want that to happen to my students, whether on a large scale or a small scale. No matter what their abilities, I want them to remain confident yet humble. Each year in

North Carolina I got my students involved in a basketball league, and at the end of each season the students voted on the most valuable player. There was one boy named Draymond who was by far the best player. However, he felt the need to regularly remind everyone how good he was. After each season, he was so angry when he wasn't voted the most valuable player. The award always went to more humble players who truly appreciated playing on a team.

I tell my students that sometimes it is hard for people to stand back and not talk about their abilities, but if they can, it will make their skills seem much greater when they are realized by others. Draymond didn't need to tell everyone how good he was at basketball; that was obvious. He should have just focused on playing his heart out and let his performance speak for itself. That is the message I try to deliver to my students.

I also spend time talking to my students about how to lose gracefully. One of my biggest pet peeves is when someone loses a game and they say something like, "I wasn't playing that hard anyway," or, "I let you win that one."

My father, Ronnie Clark, is good at every type of competition you can come up with. He is great at darts, pool, horseshoes, cards, you name it. Occasionally, however, he has had the rare misfortune of losing to me. Granted, this doesn't occur often, but it does happen. I have always tried my hardest against him, but after each game I won, he always made comments like, "Yeah, I took it easy on you that game," or, "You didn't think I was trying, did you?" It used to drive me crazy! Now, after much frustration, we have a rule in our house and in my classroom: in any competition, we will always try our best, and will never make an excuse for why we lost to someone. It makes things so much nicer, and it makes playing a lot more fun and stress free. It has almost gotten to a point where it doesn't matter who wins or loses, because we know that we try our best and we enjoy each other's efforts, no matter what the final outcome of the game.

## RULE 6

*If you are asked a question in conversation, ask a question in return. For example:*
>    *Me: "Did you have a nice weekend?"*
>    *You: "Yes, I had a great time. My family and*
>    *I went shopping. What about you? Did*
>    *you have a nice weekend?"*
*    It is only polite to show others that you are just as interested in them as they are in you.*

This is a skill that takes a while to learn. Actually, I have met many adults who have yet to master it, and, in all honesty, many never will. I tell my students that when they are talking to someone, they should make sure not to monopolize the conversation. We have all encountered that person who just won't shut up, and I don't want any of my students to grow up to be that type of person. I want them to understand that you are far more likable and respectful when you ask about the thoughts and opinions of others. It is simply an easy way to let someone know that you are interested in who they are and what they have to say.

When students walk into my classroom, I usually say something like, "Good morning, Terry, how was your weekend?" and he will respond, "Great, Mr. Clark, I went to the beach with my cousins." Then Terry will just run off to his seat. I always call the student back and tell him, "Hey, I just showed interest in what you did this weekend, and instead of showing me the same courtesy, you just ran off to your seat. Let's do that again. Terry, how was your weekend?" Terry will then respond, "Great, Mr. Clark, I went to the beach with my cousins. How was your weekend?" For kids, this takes a lot of practice, but the outcome is worth it.

Asking questions is also a skill that comes in handy when being interviewed. When my Harlem students went for their interviews to get into Manhattan East, an academically challenging junior high school, the admissions coordinator asked them who some of their favorite authors were. Many of my kids told me that after they named their favorites, they also asked the interviewer, "Do you have any authors you are particularly interested in reading?" It shows a higher level of consciousness on the part of the child and shows they are aware that the other person has interests, such as reading, as well. The same applies not just for interviews, but for any conversation.

This rule is about letting people know you are interested in them, and the results you get when you do that. When I first started working at Snowden Elementary School in North

Carolina, I made sure to spend time talking to my students about the things they were interested in. I asked them about their likes and dislikes and what they did for fun. I wanted them to know I cared about who they were, and that I wasn't there just to teach them out of a book.

In my first year of teaching there was a student named Jayson who was having a birthday party at his grandparents' trailer during the weekend. Jayson invited me, along with almost every other teacher in the school, but when I asked around, I found out no other teacher was going. I told Jayson I would be there, and I had kids asking me every five minutes if I was really going. That Saturday, even though I thought I had convinced them of my intentions, I don't think any of those kids expected me to pull up in that driveway. When I did, they all flooded around me like I was some kind of celebrity. We played freeze tag and hide-and-seek and had an incredible time. That day went a long way in terms of developing a relationship with the students and getting them to trust me. The next Monday, when I asked the kids to behave and pay attention, there was a different look in their eyes. They respected me and they listened. There are many ways to show interest in others, from being an active listener and unselfish conversationalist to making special efforts to show others you care about them. The bottom line is that it gets results.

## RULE 7

*When you cough or sneeze or burp, it is appropriate to turn your head away from others and cough into the bend of your arm. You may also use your hand if it is covered with a tissue. Using a fist is not acceptable. Afterward, you should say, "Excuse me."*

This one seems so simple, but it is surprising how many kids have never been told to do this. Actually, I notice adults all the time who cough and sneeze in public without covering their mouth. I absolutely hate riding the subway during cold and flu season because it is inevitable that someone is going to stand right behind me and cough or sneeze on my neck. Once I watched a lady sneeze on a shorter lady standing beside her, and it was like one of those slow-motion commercials. Spit and vapor formed a cloud around her face and fell like a blanket on the shorter lady. I remember thinking to myself, *Have mercy, that poor woman just caught Ebola.*

One important thing I point out to the kids is that if they frequently sneeze or cough, they should wash their hands as often as possible. Otherwise, they will pass those germs along to everything and everyone they touch.

In order to help the kids remember this rule, I tell them about an old superstition: when you sneeze, evil spirits jump into your body. If you don't cover your mouth, the spirits enter, but if you cover your mouth, you keep them out. We say, "God bless you," when someone sneezes, and in Germany you are supposed to say, "Gesundheit." That means, "Good health to you." Both expressions are said just in case you didn't cover your mouth in time and the spirits were able to enter your body. The kids love finding out the origins of these expressions and it inspires them to put the advice to use more often.

## RULE 8

*Do not smack your lips, tsk, roll your eyes, or show disrespect with gestures.*

So much time and trouble is saved by getting this rule out of the way. I doubt there is a person in America who hasn't had someone smack their lips (the sound is also known as "tsk") or roll their eyes at him or her at one time or another. Kids, especially teenagers, love to do it, but I have been able to eliminate it entirely from my classes just by pointing it out and making a rule that it will not happen in my classroom. On the first day of school, I ask if anyone in the class can smack their lips really well. I usually get more than a few students who are willing to demonstrate. I then get students to demonstrate rolling their eyes.

We then, as a class, combine the two, and we all smack and roll at the same time. It is usually a lot of fun, and I always have a few students, the pros, who turn in a good jerk of the neck and a few finger snaps. I talk to the students about how it is a form of disrespect, and that sometimes you don't have to say a single word in order to get yourself in a lot of trouble.

After that discussion, we are ready to role-play. I tell a student I am going to reprimand her for not paying attention and that I want her to smack her lips and roll her eyes. I tell her that I am then going to ask her to put her name on the board, and I want her to smack and roll as she does it. The role-play continues, and after the student has received two checks, I ask her, "So, if this had really happened, what would have been your punishment?" She responds, "I would have received a detention." I then ask, "What would have happened to the other students? Nothing. What would have happened to me? Nothing, because I'm certainly not serving a detention. So, by smacking your lips, the only person you hurt is yourself. If you had just said, 'Put my name on the board? Right away, sir,' and approached the board with a smile, then you would have only gotten your name on the board and there wouldn't have been any consequences."

By explaining it clearly to the students, you see it resonate on their faces. At RCA, when visitors watch our class, occasionally they ask me to explain how the "reward board" works. They honestly think I'm sending the students to the board for doing something right because they seem so joyful when they add their names to the board. But it's really because they know that being gracious about being disciplined means they will not experience further consequences. Making sure the kids know exactly what is expected of them in terms of their gestures and attitude, and ensuring they are aware of the consequences for those behaviors, is the best way to avoid those actions.

# RULE 9

*Always say thank you when given something. If you do not say it within three seconds after receiving the item, I will take it back. There is no excuse for not showing appreciation.*

In my opinion, this one is major. I cannot tell you the count-less times I have had to take things away from students who forgot to say thank you. They're always surprised at the begin-ning of the year at what happens when I hand out cookies at lunch or homework passes and students forget to say thank you. I take the item back, and they honestly believe I am just joking and that I'm going to wait a few seconds and then give them a second try. It never happens. For this rule to work, you have to enforce it, and sometimes that is difficult. Once, a student, along with four other kids, won a set of books for having the highest score on a social studies test. The little girl was so excited that she was jumping up and down. Others in the class quickly pointed out that she forgot to say thank you, and I had to take the books away from her. It broke my heart, but once I went with the rule, I couldn't turn back; I had to remain consistent. The kids understood that and rarely complained when I took things away from them. They knew it was a rule, and I had stated explicitly the way it worked from day one.

I recently talked with a twelfth-grade teacher at a local high school in North Carolina. She walked up to me and said she had been wanting to meet me for some time. She said she often gives treats or rewards to her seniors, and there was a group of boys in her class who always made a point to say thank you. She said one day she commented on how polite they were, and that they told her they had to be polite because their fifth-grade teacher drilled it into them. She said one boy recalled how one day he had won a lollipop, but before he could put it in his mouth, Mr. Clark had taken it away because he hadn't said thank you. He said Mr. Clark then put the lollipop in his own mouth and, with a big grin, went back to teaching. That stuck in his mind, and he swore he would never forget to say thank you again.

In my day-to-day life, I always try to make sure to thank whoever I am dealing with—the checkout clerk, the waitress, a person who holds the door for me, the friend who does a favor or anyone who does something for me, no matter how major or minor. At my school in Harlem, the custodian occasionally mopped and cleaned our rooms during the night shift. I was always so pleasantly surprised when I walked into my freshly cleaned room, and I made a point to thank him several times for doing such good work. He always seemed surprised I was thanking him for just doing his job. I could tell he appreciated it, though, and I started to notice that my room was mopped and cleaned a lot more often.

When I took the subway to work in New York City, Monday mornings meant I had to stand in a long line to get my week's worth of tokens. (Back in the dark ages, tokens were coin-like objects humans used to be granted access to the train.) The token lady at my subway stop always looked like she had just swallowed a lemon, and I hated having to deal with her first thing every Monday. She never spoke to anyone, she just had this grimace on her face, took the money, and shoved the tokens toward the customers. Well, I was determined to get her to be nice to me. Each and every Monday morning, I said to her, "Good morning," with no response. I then ended with, "Thank you," and again, there would be no response. I kept at it, however, even though on the inside I just wanted to say, "Excuse me, are you aware that you are the rudest person on earth?" One day, after several weeks of this, when I said, "Thank you," she replied, "You're welcome." I almost fell over. The next person in line approached the window to order, but I jumped back and said, "What did you say?" She looked shocked, and she said, "You're welcome," and she smiled at me. From then on, my Monday morning subway experiences were pleasant...well, as pleasant as a Monday morning subway experience can be.

## RULE 10

*When you are given something from someone, never insult that person by making negative comments about the gift or by insinuating that it wasn't appreciated.*

One month I took all of the top readers in the class to a Charlotte Hornets pro basketball game. They stayed overnight in a hotel, met the players, and had a blast at the game. The following month, the top readers were going to be rewarded with a trip to the local bowling alley. The disparity was hard to miss, and it definitely didn't go unnoticed by the students. They were vocal about the difference in the trips, and it really hurt my feelings. Most teachers didn't take their students on any trips at all, yet mine complained the bowling trip wasn't as nice as the previous month's trip. To teach them a lesson, I canceled the bowling trip and gave them no reward. It may seem harsh to cancel the trip, but it was a very effective way to get my point across to the ungrateful students, and hopefully the memory of why they were punished is a lasting one.

Sometimes people miss opportunities in life because they are ungrateful, but they aren't even aware of what they are missing. Upon graduating eighth grade at RCA, sixty percent of our students receive scholarships to attend the nation's premier boarding schools. Most of our students, however, have never even stepped foot on a boarding school campus, and so we decided to take our entire eighth grade on a trip to visit several of the institutions. We divided the groups into five students and one chaperone each, and each group then made the trip to visit a different set of schools over a two-day period. The parents were so grateful and many sent us emails thanking us from the bottom of their hearts for exposing their children to the schools. The next year we decided to do the trip again with our new eighth graders, but the parents didn't send emails of appreciation. They saw the class the year before had gone on the trip so I guess they didn't feel the need to say, "Thank you," for something that was now expected. The third year, not only did they not say thank you, but parents complained they weren't happy with the schools their child would visit and asked to have them switched to other chaperones' groups so that they could experience different schools. It honestly upset my staff, who were taking time from their families to make the trip with the students. Instead of showing appreciation, the parents showed entitlement, and it led our staff to the point where many wanted to cancel the trips altogether.

When I took ten of our fifth graders from RCA to stay at my parents' home in Washington, North Carolina for a few days, they were so excited and wanted to do everything correctly. I thought I had prepared them for how to show appreciation, but then something happened I hadn't planned on. After we returned home from a hayride, my mom walked out with a tray and said, "Surprise everyone. I made y'all some hot chocolate with marshmallows. Would anyone like some?" The students responded, "No, thank you," and proceeded to walk in the house. I caught Isaiah's eye and gave him a death stare, and he said, "Oh, I'll drink some," but the rest of the students were already heading upstairs. My mother just responded, "Oh me, maybe they'd rather have milk or something else to drink." She's so darn sweet.

I proceeded upstairs and gathered the students and explained how rude it was not to take the hot chocolate. One girl responded, "But I don't like hot chocolate," and one of the boys said, "My mom said not to drink anything before I went to bed." I had to explain to them that in that situation my mom was giving them a gift and that they should have accepted it with joy. I explained they could have just had a little and then thrown it away when my mom wasn't looking but to just say no and walk away after she had worked hard to prepare it wasn't acceptable.

It's irritating to give a gift that's not appreciated, but anytime someone goes out of their way to do something for you, that should be seen as a gift as well. Appreciation and acceptance of the gift should follow suit.

## RULE 11

*Surprise others by performing random acts of kindness. Go out of your way to do something surprisingly kind and generous for someone at least once a month.*

All of the kids love this rule; it sounds as if it is a really good idea and that it would be a lot of fun. The problem is that it is one of the hardest rules for people to follow. In our daily lives, we get so busy and preoccupied that there isn't much time to sit down and think up a surprise for someone. Usually, if it isn't someone's birthday or a special occasion, people really don't see a need to go out of their way to do something special for someone else. I feel, however, that the best time to give someone a nice surprise is when it isn't expected. That way, the person knows you didn't do it because of obligation, you did it because you wanted to.

The types of surprises I'm talking about are more than just getting someone a gift. These surprises need to be more thought out and meaningful. For example, take the time to make a lunch, complete with salad, entrée, and dessert, and set it up in a room where you work. Place flowers on the table and play some soft music in the background. Then invite the custodians to take a break and enjoy the lunch you prepared for them. Or, when your neighbors are at work, mow their lawn and clip their hedges. I tell my students they can clean their entire room, vacuum the house or do the dishes without being asked to. They can do errands or read to an elderly neighbor or they can take someone fresh flowers. The opportunities are all around.

Each year, we take our sixth-grade class to Salt Lake City to learn how to ski. One of our donors, Jeff Anderson, and his family host us in their home and it's always a magical experience. One year, a student took a gift for Mr. Anderson. I had no idea about it beforehand, but she had made him a beautiful card that was attached to homemade peach preserves. The card read, "You are sharing your home with us, so I wanted to share some of my home with you. These are peach preserves I made with my grandmother."

Mr. Anderson's family was so blown away that they invited the girl and her family to come to Salt Lake City to stay in their mountain cabin anytime they'd like. It's such a small gesture to bring a gift, but it makes an enormous impact when done the right way.

My desire to surprise others stems from how my parents constantly arranged surprises for my sister and me. We never had a lot of money, but I remember how seeing them go out of their way to do kind and unexpected things for us made me feel so special and loved. I promised myself that when I was older I was going to do similar things for all of those around me. When I became a teacher, I found myself spending hundreds of dollars a month on books, contest prizes, and many other items for the students. Small surprises like that were appreciated by the kids. But then something happened. I started a project with the kids that led to the biggest surprise I have ever been involved with. It forever changed my life and the lives of the students.

It all started when I taught a lesson on the newspaper, and the students had trouble understanding how the classified ads work. I decided to have them place their own ad in the paper so they could see firsthand how the process works. I had each child bring a nickel to contribute to the ad because I wanted to give them ownership in the project. I then instructed them to come up with an ad for the classifieds. Immediately, they wanted to place a Lexus for sale in the "Autos for Sale" section. I had to remind them, "We don't have a Lexus," to which Anton responded, "But my Uncle Leory has one. We can sell his Lexus." I quickly replied, "We are not selling your Uncle Leory's Lexus!"

We eventually decided to place a geography puzzle in the paper and ask readers to write us back with the answer. Our first puzzle stated: "What is the largest island in the world? If you know the answer, please write to our class." We included our address and anxiously waited to see if we would get a response. To our surprise, we received ten letters from different individuals around the area. The kids loved it because no one had the right answer, and they got to write each person back with the correct answer: Greenland.

The kids were so excited with the letters we received that we decided to place additional puzzles in papers across the state. Whenever we learned new information in class, the students would place questions about the content in various papers. The project became less about a lesson on the classifieds and more about what the students were learning from all the people who were writing our class. In order to get more responses, we marched in parades with banners that had questions painted on them along with a request to send answers to our school. We passed out flyers at local supermarkets and even gave a puzzle on a radio show. Soon we were receiving dozens of letters a day from people across our state—doctors, lawyers, Arabian horse farm owners, people from all kinds of professions. The letters didn't just contain the answers, however; there were words of advice, information about various hobbies, tips on how to get into college, and fascinating life stories. My students in our small town of 600 people were learning about life outside our borders.

The kids were thoroughly enjoying the project when one day a boy named Cole said, "Hey, Mr. Clark, I was thinking, we should go worldwide with this project." He meant that we should put a puzzle in a paper that goes all around the world. It sounded like a good idea to me, so I decided to send Cole to the office to call *USA Today* to find out how much a 4 × 5-inch ad would cost in their paper. (It always bothers me when I call my students' homes and they have poor phone manners, so I try to get them to make calls for me whenever possible.) I made sure Cole knew precisely what I wanted him to ask and exactly what information I expected from him. I then demonstrated a practice call with him in front of the other students, and then I sent him to make the call. When Cole returned, he placed his hands on his hips and informed me seriously in his deep southern drawl, "Mr. Clark, you better sit down." He proceeded to tell me that it was going to cost

$12,000. I didn't believe him at first, and I had to call myself after school to confirm the amount. Cole was right, and I was astounded at how much such a little ad would cost for just one day's printing in the paper.

After much discussion with the kids, I explained to them that it would be impossible for us to raise that amount of money. The students, however, were not willing to give up so easily. They begged me to let them try, and when students become excited about the learning process, I never want to squash that. Also, I had an idea that trying to raise the funds could potentially present an interesting math lesson. I didn't figure we could raise all of the money, but trying to accumulate $12,000 would present a major life lesson. Therefore, we soon began a campaign to raise the necessary funds. I told them I would do any fund-raiser they were interested in: bake sales, candy sales, anything but a car wash, because I hate car washes. That Saturday, we had a car wash.

Weeks later, our "creative" earning strategies weren't getting us very far, when I received a phone call from USA Today. Joan Baraloto, an editor for the paper, told me that someone had seen my class on TV trying to raise the money, and that he wanted to donate the $12,000 necessary for the ad. I immediately asked her the name of the person, and she told me he wanted to be known only as "Santa Claus." It was three weeks before Christmas, so it seemed to be a fitting title for such a generous contributor. I hurried to the class and informed the kids that someone had donated the money for our ad. They cheered like crazy and then asked, "Who gave us the money?" I replied with a slight grin, "Santa Claus." Cole looked at me incredulously and said, "Mr. Clark, my parents ain't got that kind of money." We eventually decided to place the following ad (this was in 1995, and the students found it appropriate to address the question to the president):

ATTENTION PRESIDENT CLINTON AND PEOPLE AROUND THE WORLD
What kills more people each year than AIDS, alcohol abuse, car accidents, murders, suicides, illegal drugs, and fires combined?

The students actually created this ad. I was a little worried about it coming from a state that produces so much tobacco (that's a hint to the answer), and I didn't want to ruffle any feathers. I mentioned that to the kids, and one girl, Carmeka, said to me, "Well, Mr. Clark, just because we come from this state doesn't mean we can't have our own opinions." She had a point.

As this occurred before we had access to the Internet and even email, we placed our address and fax number in the ad and anxiously awaited the responses.

On the day the ad appeared, I wasn't even able to get a copy of the paper because USA Today isn't delivered to our rural area. The effects of the ad were felt, however, as we had already received over 100 faxes before I even arrived at school. As I pulled into the parking lot of the school, my mild-mannered co-teacher, Barbara Jones, was in the parking lot jumping up and down and cheering. "Mr. Clark, Mr. Clark, you've got to get to the office! Stop the car, I'll park it for you!" As I ran into the office, the first fax I picked up and read was from the prime minister of Canada. There were also faxes from the cast of *Friends*, sports teams, doctors in India, and people from everywhere you can imagine.

When the students arrived at school, we took over the office! Radio shows all over the country were reading our ad on the air and asking their listeners to call in with their answers. The radio shows were then calling our school to find out what the real answer was, so there were kids on three different phone lines talking to thousands of listeners. I had kids out in the hall being interviewed by TV reporters, faxes coming in constantly from all over the world, and students about to jump through the roof with excitement! When the school day was finally over, we realized that the fax machine was going to be going all night, and that no one would be there to keep paper in the machine, and that we would lose a lot of responses. I spent the night in the school office. Faxes came in constantly throughout the entire night, and my students' parents brought me fried chicken and Coca Cola at 11 P.M. to help keep me awake.

The students loved hearing from the various individuals and to see their responses to our question. We made a bar graph down the hall and charted all of the answers. Here are some of our more common and favorite responses: starvation, guns, falls in the tub, James Bond, love, heart attack, abortion, old age, suspense, ignorance, the fifth grade, time, greed, the tongue, hangnails, puzzles. Three people faxed in "ex-wives," and when my students asked, "What does that mean, Mr. Clark?" I responded, "Maybe we'll leave that one off the graph."

We eventually received over 7,000 letters and packages from all over the world. We had promised in the ad to write each person back, so the kids had to meet on Saturdays, during holidays, and after school to hand-write each individual a response, letting each person know that the correct answer is tobacco use.

The students became local celebrities, were featured on national news programs, and appeared on the covers of newspapers across the state. A great deal of excitement surrounded the project, and the kids started to hold their heads high and come to school each day on top of the world.

After a week of writing letters, turning the school office into our own makeshift headquarters, and being the center of media attention, we finally received the answer we had been waiting for. The White House called and said that First Lady Hillary Clinton would call on Friday at 11:45 A.M. to give the president's and her answer and to discuss the dangers of tobacco use with the students. We were all elated, and rushed to set up a press conference for the end of the week so that all of the community could be in attendance for the call.

As we all sat in the library, political leaders, business owners, family, and friends, you could just feel the excitement in the air and the sense of community. We had purchased clothes so that all of the students were dressed in "Sunday clothes" and looking their best. The class and I sat at tables at the head of the library with dozens of cameras and media personalities only a few feet from our faces. I looked at the clock... 11:43... I looked again... 11:44.... Then I thought, "What if this woman doesn't call?" Then the phone rang.

The library is supposed to be quiet, but it had never been that quiet. We all held our breath as we hung on every word of the call, which was supposed to be fifteen minutes but stretched to forty-five minutes in length. Mrs. Clinton took the time to speak with each child individually and to discuss the health issues raised by our question. At the end of the call, Mrs. Clinton said, "You know, I've got this letter here that the president and I wrote to your class that includes our answer, and we could mail it to you, but we would much rather give it to you in person." Then I made an announcement that shocked everyone. I had been talking with the White House all week, and we had arranged for the students to actually go to the White House the following week to meet with the First Family. This was going to be a life-changing event for the students, as most of them had never even left our state. When we were first informed about the ensuing invitation to the White House, the principal asked me not to make the trip public knowledge until I had enough funding to take all of the students. We knew it was going to take quite a bit of effort. Immediately, Mrs. Austin, one of the secretaries at the school, and I began calling every business we could think of to try to get donations. I discovered quickly that no matter who I called, they were interested in helping kids and were willing to contribute to helping in any way they could. I have found that true no matter where I have taught; communities are willing to help teachers, as long as you can show you are hardworking and can give solid reasons for how the contributions can make a difference. I simply look people in the eye and say, "I need your help and it's for the kids." Within a few days, funding for the entire trip had been obtained from local business owners.

At the end of the phone call, in response to Mrs. Clinton's request for us to go to the White House, I said, through tears that I could not suppress no matter how hard I tried, "Kids, you see this community of business leaders around you... well, they have been kind enough to make contributions to our class, and next week WE'RE ALL GOING TO WASHINGTON, D.C.!!" The library erupted with applause. I was crying, the students and their parents were crying, Shanae Harris from Channel 9 was crying. Delivering that surprise to those students and that community was one of the most amazing moments of my life. The joy, excitement, and appreciation on the faces of those students is one of the main reasons I decided to continue teaching. How could I turn my back on the opportunity to have that kind of an impact on the lives of children?

After the excitement of the announcement calmed down, I began organizing the trip. I expected it was going to be overwhelming, but once I started making calls, obtaining hotel reservations, and jotting out an itinerary, everything just seemed to fall into place. It does take effort for such an undertaking, but I just relied on the advice of those around me whom I trusted, and I made sure I tried to cover every possible detail.

The following week we made the trip to D.C., along with reporters from local newspapers. As we were about thirty miles from our town, one of the students who had rarely traveled anywhere said with wide eyes, "Mr. Clark, I don't think we are in Aurora anymore."

Once we arrived in the nation's capital, we visited the National Symphony Orchestra, the Capitol building, and all of the major museums. The last day of our time in D.C. we made our trip to the White House. A guide gave us a personal tour, and we were the only ones there. We were allowed to roam free, take pictures, and make ourselves at home. One of the highlights of the visit was the bathroom, because the toilet tissue had a picture of the White House on every sheet. Later, when we left, I said to the parents who were chaperones, "Did any of you use the restroom at the White House?" and they responded, "Yeah, we all did." I then added, "Did you notice how highfalutin it was that they have a picture of the White House on each of the sheets of toilet tissue?" Mr. Farrow, a parent, responded, "Yeah, I know. I took me a roll"—and he pulled it out of his bag.

After our tour, we were led to the East Room; it was decorated with a huge Christmas tree with lights everywhere. Finally, the president and Mrs. Clinton entered the room and began talking to the kids. President Clinton read the students "'Twas the Night Before Christmas," and then we all sang Christmas carols. When we were done, the president actually knelt on the floor to talk to each child and Mrs. Clinton went around and talked to the adults. When she walked over to me, she said, "Oh, Mr. Clark, I recognize you from the newspapers," and I replied, "Oh, Mrs. Clinton, I recognize you from TV."

When the kids and I returned to North Carolina, they didn't want the project to end. To keep it alive a little longer, we wrote a book about the entire project called *An Adventure Around the World Through the Words of Others*. The students had so many feelings and memories tied in with that project, and I feel so fortunate that we were able to capture those feelings in time by collecting them all and placing them in writing. It's now been decades since that book was published and the students from that class have let me know they have since read the book to their children. It was such a magical experience, and I hope as they share the journey with their children that those old emotions come to life again and again.

That was a once-in-a-lifetime experience, but I was lucky enough to have a similar experience with my students in Harlem. Each year, Disney sponsors the American Teacher Awards. In my second year in New York City, I found out I was a finalist for the Outstanding Teacher of the Year Award and that I was supposed to fly to Los Angeles in November for the final stages of the competition. I told the people at Disney that I would really love to bring my class with me. They informed me that Disney could not help me financially, but if I could raise the money I was more than welcome to bring my students.

I didn't want to get the students' hopes up, so I didn't tell them what I was trying to do. Instead, I went around to businesses throughout New York City and I wrote over 100 letters to business owners. Thanks to the efforts of students' parents and the assistant principal, Mrs. Castillo, who spent days on the phone arranging funding and finding sponsors, small amounts of money started to come in. Then, one day I got a phone call from a student's mother, Mrs. Miriam Vazquez, who told me that the law firm where she worked, Morrison & Foerster, was so touched by the attempt to take all of the students on the trip that they were going to contribute the remaining $16,000 needed to make the trip possible. I was thrilled! I immediately called a night meeting for all of my students and their parents in the auditorium. I told them that we had raised enough money so that a few students could go on the trip and that we were going to put all of their names in a fishbowl and draw out the names of the three lucky students. I said to the group, "As you know, I am going to Los Angeles next month, and you have all been very wonderful and supportive. Well, I want you to know that when I go, I won't be alone. We have received enough donations so that I will be taking a few very special students with me, and we are here tonight to determine who they will be. As you see I have this fishbowl with all of your names in it." I then placed my hand in the bowl and started to twirl the names around, and you could just see the anticipation on all of the students' faces. I then stopped and said, "But you know, actually there is no need for me to do the drawing, because, kids, we have raised enough money, and next month we're all going on the trip to Los Angeles!!"

It was an electric moment. I expected the kids to explode with joy like the students in North Carolina. Their parents did, but many of the kids just put their faces in their hands and started crying. I think they were overwhelmed and relieved that they were all going to make the trip. It was obvious that the opportunity to go on a once-in-a-lifetime trip meant a great deal to them.

I know it is impossible to arrange surprises like that for people every month, but I think we should all try to capture that type of excitement by giving some type of surprise, whether it is large or small, as often as possible. For me, teaching is about making surprises and moments for kids that they will never forget. It would be much more fun to live in a world where everyone thought that way.

## RULE 12

*Occasionally we may grade each other's papers as a group. When grading other students' papers, if you give someone an incorrect grade, whether it is higher or lower than they deserve, the amount the grade differs from the actual grade will be deducted from your paper. The only marks you are allowed to make on others' papers are an "X" and the number they got incorrect.*

As adults, we are always put in situations where we have to look at the performance of others and make judgments. We do it constantly on the job, whether we are interviewing candidates, evaluating our coworkers, or choosing our business partners. We are able to learn a lot about ourselves and the level of achievement we should expect by observing the way our peers operate. Assessing others and letting them know your summation of their abilities can be very challenging, however, because you must have a great deal of confidence in yourself in order to do so. You must feel secure with your own performance before you can tell others what is right or wrong with how they have performed. Teaching students to evaluate the work of their peers in the classroom, and having them practice appropriate techniques of delivering feedback, prepares them for what they are going to face later in life.

Unfortunately, some school systems do not allow students to grade each other's papers because it can be a social embarrassment for students who aren't doing well. If not done under the right supervision and in the right type of classroom environment, I agree with that sentiment. However, if you create a supportive atmosphere where students feel comfortable with others knowing their scores, then the sharing of grades can be very helpful and go a long way toward motivating students.

First of all, having students grade each other's papers is quick and offers immediate feedback to the teacher. The main problem is that students' feelings may be hurt; therefore, I often have the students leave off their name on their papers. After I teach a lesson, I have the students take out a sheet of paper. I then ask them anywhere from five to ten questions, and I have them pass up their papers. I immediately turn around and pass the papers back out, so that no one knows exactly whose paper they have. I give the answers, and then I have the students raise their hands for perfect scores, minus one, minus two, and so on. This gives me a good, and immediate, indication of the class's mastery of what I have taught. Having the students grade each other's papers, therefore, served its purpose and didn't embarrass any of the students. For times when no names have been placed on papers, I just collect them back from the students and chuck them in the recycling; there is no need to keep them around, because I already got the feedback I needed.

There are times, however, when I want to have a more

specific idea of how each child is doing, so I do have the students write their names on the papers. After they have been checked, I have the students hold on to the papers they checked. I then ask them to raise their hands to designate the number of questions missed before they pass the papers back. This spares a student the humiliation of having to raise her own hand to show that she has a low score.

Sometimes, I have students who graded a paper with a perfect score call out the names of the individuals who performed so well.

Before you have a class grade papers with the names on each paper, there are two things I would make sure to discuss:

1. Tell the students that privacy is required at all times when grading someone else's paper. Tell them they are not to comment on the other student's grade, not to that student or any other student in the class.

2. When grading, the students are only to mark Xs for incorrect answers and a final tally at the top of the paper showing how many were wrong. This is important, because you will have some students who will get carried away and write things on the papers like "You go, girl!" or, "Lord knows you did bad," or, "What were you thinking?" Those are all actual comments I have seen students write on papers in the past. Limiting what they can put on the paper will also keep them from being able to change answers. If you are going over the answers with the class and you see a student writing words, you will know something is up

because there is no reason for them to be writing anything on the paper other than an X.

## RULE 13

*When we read together in class, you must follow along. If I call on you to read, you must know exactly where we are and begin reading immediately.*

I can remember sitting in classes as a student while we read together as a group. Sometimes, out of boredom, I would stare at the page we were on and daydream about anything from winning the lottery to being asked by NASA to be the first high school student to fly to the Moon. I seldom paid attention to the details of the text, but I always managed to get the general gist of what was being read. It just didn't excite me enough to command my full attention.

As an adult, I find myself in numerous meetings where I have that same type of boredom, and I just shut down and don't pay attention to what is going on. To get through it, I force myself to be an active participant. I think of questions to ask, make comments, and take notes. I try to make the most of the time I have to spend in any particular meeting, because I have to be there anyway. Many times, I do not even have the opportunity to make my comments or ask my questions, but just getting in the mindset that I might be speaking or raising my hand at any second makes my heart race a little faster, and I pay attention. I try to get my kids to learn to be active participants. I try to get them to stay on task, following along in the books we read and preparing themselves to make comments or ask questions throughout the lessons. No one in my class is going to slouch down and stare out the window. We all stay focused and are part of the lesson and discussions.

When reading together, having everyone on task and attentive at all times can be unrealistic and almost impossible to achieve. I have found that the subject students find most boring is reading. Some students just absolutely hate it; especially silent reading. I was once reading a chapter of *The Indian in the Cupboard* with my class, and I stopped and asked them to continue reading silently. I turned and began writing the homework on the board; soon I sensed someone was standing behind me. I turned and there was a little boy named Drew looking up at me with a very content expression. I said, "What is it, Drew?" and he said, "I finished that reading, Mr. Clark." Drew wasn't a very good reader, and I knew there was no way he could have finished the entire chapter. I said, "You did!" and he said, grinning from ear to ear, "Yep, I read the *whole* page." I just looked at him, raised an eyebrow, and said with a smirk, "Now, Drew..." and he replied in an embarrassed way, "Oooooh, I'm sorry, Mr. Clark, you wanted us to read the front AND the back of the page," and he turned and trotted off to his seat. I didn't have the heart to tell him I expected him to finish reading the whole chapter.

My point of mentioning my daydreaming in high school and Drew's misunderstanding is that reading and staying on task can be a real struggle. I mean, you are going to have students who just love to read. They are going to be attentive with little effort on the part of the teacher. It is the students who dread reading and have difficulties with it that I try to reach when doing reading with my class. There are several strategies I use together with my rule about following along as we read as a class.

## Strategy 1

When I read with my students, I read with force, energy, and expression. I try to let go of all inhibitions and "become" the character. Sometimes while reading I'll jump on a student's desk, jump over to another desk, scream at the top of my lungs or fall to the floor. Anything I can do to make the reading more dramatic and to take the students to that place in the story, I do it. I have a thousand different voices I use, and there are times when I finish part of a reading passage and the kids break into applause. They genuinely appreciate my efforts to bring the readings to life and to make the story exciting. The way I read transfers to my students as well, as they, too, read with expression and have character voices of their own. It makes the whole experience more enjoyable, and it teaches them how captivating reading can be.

## Strategy 2

I try to select readings I think are enchanting, appealing, and full of intriguing characters. One of the main tests I use when selecting readings is to ask myself if it is something I would enjoy. If the answer is no, I pick something else. I hear kids all the time talk about how they don't like to read. I always tell them that perhaps they just aren't reading the right things for them.

## Strategy 3

This is where Rule 13 takes effect. If the readings I have selected are entertaining and if we are reading them as a class with energy and expression, then the students have no reason not to pay attention as we are reading. Therefore, I have the rule that if I see that a student's eyes are not on the page as we are reading or if I call on a student to read and he or she doesn't know where we are, that child's name will be placed on the board. In the beginning, I always have to place several names on the board. Some students prefer to watch my facial expressions rather than follow the words on the page, and it takes a while to teach them to "see" the story in their minds. Also, there is a time set aside each day when I read to the kids out of a novel, and they aren't required to follow along. That helps them develop their listening comprehension skills and gives them the opportunity to "watch the show."

Why is it so important to have the students follow along when we read together? First of all, as we read, they see new words and hear their pronunciations, which adds to their word recognition and vocabulary base. It also helps them observe the appropriate rhythmic flow of text. Most important, I am training them to learn to focus as they read and comprehend as they go along.

If you have struggling readers or those with disabilities such as dyslexia, you should always be sensitive to that. With those students at RCA, I often meet with them one-on-one to get their opinion on reading in front of the group. Many are uncomfortable at first, and so I tell them that instead of calling on them to read, I will ask them to give their opinion on what is happening in the story. In that way, I can make sure they are following along. To encourage them to eventually read aloud, I let them know the paragraph I'd like them to read a couple of days ahead of time. This gives them the opportunity to practice at home so they will have more confidence and be familiar with the passage.

## RULE 14

*Answer all written questions with a complete sentence. For example, if the question asks, "What is the capital of Russia?" you should respond by writing, "The capital of Russia is Moscow." Also, in conversation with others, it is important to use complete sentences out of respect for the person's question. For example, if a person asks, "How are you?" instead of just responding by saying, "Fine," you should say, "I'm doing fine, thank you. How about yourself?"*

This rule helps students develop a command of the written language. It helps them learn to develop and organize their thoughts, especially when the questions require a short but thought-out answer. For example, the question, "Do you feel the proposal to add forty-five minutes to the school day should be passed?" might be answered with a "No" without any explanation unless kids are taught to answer their questions in-depth and with complete thoughts.

My co-teacher in North Carolina, Barbara Jones, taught math and science, but she did a wonderful job of integrating writing into her subjects. She had her students keep a math journal, and in it they would explain, in writing, the way they solved various problems. She always asked that they begin their answer by restating the question and using complete sentences. This was an excellent way to integrate subjects, and, as the students' writing teacher, I appreciated the extra effort she took to work with them on their writing skills.

Each year in North Carolina the fifth graders are given an open-ended assessment test. They are asked to read a passage and then respond to short-answer questions about the text. At times, I had nonreaders and students far below grade level in my class. When working on writing, however, I would always instruct them to answer their questions in the following way:

**Example question:**

Of the basketball players, who do you think was better, Lloyd or Jason?

1. **Restate the question and give your answer:**
   Of the basketball players, I think that Lloyd was better.

2. **Give a reason why you feel that way:**
   I think Lloyd was better because he made the winning shot.

3. **Support your answer:**
   Since he made the winning shot, it shows he stayed calm under pressure and he was determined to win.

4. **Restate the question and close:**
   Therefore, I think that Lloyd was a better player than Jason.

After much work and development of that basic outline, my students soon learned to write well-developed, thought-out answers to any question. After mastering this technique, many of my students are able to use this outline to write more creative and elaborate answers, but their answers retain the organization needed to make their writing top-notch. Even my nonreaders find the outline easy to learn and they find success with it as well.

In my first year, I had only been with the class three weeks before the open-ended test, and many of the nonreaders just sat and stared at the test and wrote nothing. It broke my heart, but all I could do was smile and tell them to try their best. I taught both fifth grade classes at the school, and we scored dead last in the county. The next year, I was determined that our scores would rise. I developed the writing outline, and we worked on it throughout the year in all subjects. When the test results came back, every fifth grader at my school passed the test, and our school scored first in the county. I even had students who were reading on a first grade level pass the test, because they had learned to restate the question, give an answer, give support to that answer, and restate for a closing.

The key to not only pass the test but to receive the highest marks, however, is to teach the students to "go deeper." This is something we start first with our conversations and then translate it to our writing. For example, when we practice how to be a good conversationalist, I encourage the students to latch onto a topic and dive deep. A conversation may go like this:

> **Student:** "What are your favorite hobbies?"
> **Adult:** "I really like soccer."
> (At this point, the student dives for more information.)
> **Student:** "Oh, really? Do you play on a team or coach soccer?"

When students are first learning, they ask questions like, "Do you use a soccer ball?" It's a crisis, but with more practice they get better at it. Then when we are writing, I explain that we want to dive deep into our writing in the same way we do our conversations. The process not only helps them with their interpersonal skills, but it also adds depth and vibrant details to their written passages.

# RULE 15

*At times throughout the year, I will give rewards for good behavior, academic performance, and other acts worthy of praise. If you ever ask me for a reward, however, it will not be given. It is rude to ask if you are getting something for good behavior. You should be good and try your best because you are trying to better yourself, not because you are anticipating a reward. I usually give some sort of reward to everyone who scores 100 on unit tests. If you make 100 and ask if you are getting something, no one who made 100 will be given anything.*

At work in the real world, rewards aren't always given to people for a job well done. People do a good job because they take pride in their performance, they love what they do, and/or they want to keep their jobs. Even though I reward my students often, I know I have to prepare them for what life is going to be like after the classroom. I try to get them to perform and realize it is important to do well not for a reward but for themselves.

I really go out of the way to reward my students and praise them for their work, but it got to a point where I felt as if the kids were going from being appreciative for the things I was giving them to a point where they'd say, "What are we getting next?" Once I passed reports back to the class, and a little girl who got the highest grade said, "Mr. Clark, am I getting anything?" From that moment on, I put an end to comments like

that. I made sure the class understood that under no circumstances were they ever to ask me for any type of reward or if
they were getting anything. The students still might have felt
a bit greedy on the inside, but I was going to make sure that
at least their actions did not reflect it. Over time, I hoped that
learning to accept what is given without expecting and asking
for rewards would sink in and change their attitudes toward
the benefits of a good, individual performance.

Even after I told the students this rule, they would occasionally still slip up. One time I stayed up late making homemade chocolate chip cookies for the kids who would pass the
next day's unit test on the Revolutionary War. After I passed
back the tests, Queshida said, "Mr. Clark, do we get anything
for doing good on the test?" You could have heard a pin drop
in the class. There were big eyes all over the classroom, and
mine were the biggest! I was livid, because I had stayed up
for hours making those darn cookies...okay, it took me five
minutes to slice them off the roll, but nevertheless, I knew
that I couldn't give them out after she had asked for them. If I
did, I would be going back on my word and ignoring the rule.
I simply said, "Well, I did have these chocolate chip cookies
for you"—I paused and tasted one—"but since you asked,
no one will get them." I walked across the hall and gave the
cookies to Ms. Hopkins to share with her class. Not a single
student in that class ever asked me about a reward again.
It's a hard lesson to learn, but if it helps the kids learn to
appreciate their efforts over their rewards, it will have been
worth it.

## RULE 16

*Homework will be turned in each day for each subject by every student with no exceptions.*

As adults, we are used to deadlines, due dates, and the pressure of being on time. We have to pay bills by a certain date, turn in assignments, and complete tasks quickly and efficiently. When I talk to my students about their work and what is required of them, I approach it from the standpoint that the work is part of the students' job. I want them to learn to be on time and proficient at a young age.

One way that I do that is by expecting every student to have every piece of homework every day. This is a nearly impossible task, right? Well, not really. If managed correctly, you can have every child in the classroom completing all assignments and turning them in on time, but it takes some effort. There are three things I do to make it happen.

**First** *is detention.* If a child does not do a homework assignment, he or she is given a detention slip and is expected to stay after school for an hour the following day to do additional work. This is effective, but you can't expect results on punishment alone. If all you do is punish, you won't get good results.

**Second**, *I keep a homework tally banner.* I keep a huge sign outside the classroom that tracks how many days in a row all the students in the class have done all their homework assignments. It is a simple sign that states:

### EVERY STUDENT IN THIS CLASS HAS COMPLETED HIS/HER HOMEWORK FOR _____ DAYS IN A ROW.

Each day, after checking to see that each child has their work, I change the total. The kids love it, and it is a very positive motivator. For the first ten days in a row, the students get no reward; however, for each day *after* the ten in a row the class continues to complete each and every homework assignment, I cook something for them at night and give it to them at lunchtime. For example, on the eleventh day I might have cookies, the twelfth day it might be brownies. You are probably saying, "Good grief, this crazy man is cooking each night for those kids!" But this is the way I see it: I have *every* kid in my class intent on completing each assignment correctly. (And I give quite a bit of homework, by the way.) All I have to do is dump a box of mix in a bowl, bake it, cut it into squares, and take it to school. I don't think that is a lot to ask when you are getting such wonderful results from the entire class. The record for days in a row stands at sixty-two. I was a baking fool that year. That was my first year in Harlem, and those kids went from thirty percent homework participation to 100 percent, and their end-of-year test scores were through the roof. I know a great part of that was because of their diligence and consistency with the work they completed at home.

**Third**, *I use peer pressure.* As you can probably imagine, the class was not too thrilled when a student would forget their homework and cause the class to have to go all the way back to "0 Days in a Row." In fact, I never had to reprimand the child who broke the streak. The weight of having broken the streak was usually enough to bear. Actually, the amount of pressure I let the other kids apply depended on the individual student.

Take Jarron. When he broke the streak, he didn't seem to mind. That was just his attitude. He was very carefree and seemed unconcerned with ruining it for the entire class. Well, I let the class lay it on thick. I saw them glare at him, I watched them fuss at him at lunchtime, I saw them reminding him of what the homework assignment was...and I said nothing. I knew he could take the heat, and eventually, it did get him back on track.

Take Alison. The comments from the rest of the class would only annoy her and, in fact, have a negative impact. She had the attitude that she wasn't going to do the homework just because everyone was bugging her to do it. Therefore, if she didn't complete her work, I told the class to leave her alone because if they started bugging her, I knew there was no way she would do it. When she was left alone, there was a far greater chance of her doing her work.

Take Rubina, the best and most prepared student in the class. She cared what her classmates thought of her, and she would rather eat nails than disappoint me. She was the sweetest, hardest-working student...and she was the student who broke the streak of sixty-two days in a row. By the time I got to her desk to check to see if she had her work, her face was covered in tears. It had been a mistake, a mistake anyone could have made. Rubina was responsible for helping her other siblings get ready for school, and in the rush out of her home, she had left her worksheets on the table beside her bed. I knew instantly she didn't have the work, so I walked to the front of the room and I said, "Class, we need to have a talk. We all know that Rubina is one of the most dedicated and hardworking students in this class. She has given her all to make sure this class made it to the streak of sixty-two, and even though the streak will end today at sixty-two, I think we as a class need to give ourselves *and* Rubina a round of applause, because I am telling you right now, I bet there is no class *in this nation* that finished their homework sixty-two days in a row this year, and we have a lot to be proud of." Of course, no punishment went to Rubina; it wasn't necessary. How some situations are handled depends a lot on the child.

## RULE 17

*When we are in transition from one subject to the other, the change will be swift, quiet, and orderly. We should be consistently able to turn from one book to another, complete with all homework and necessary materials, as quickly as possible. The opportune amount of time to spend in transition should be less than ten seconds, and we will work toward a goal of seven seconds.*

In our daily lives, we are faced with multiple tasks we must accomplish. Often, instead of completing all of the tasks in an orderly fashion, we are interrupted by distractions such as the telephone, that tempting TV show, that comfy couch, or conversations with coworkers. We could be so much more efficient if we could just stick to our goals, complete them, and use the remaining time for our leisure activities. I try very hard to get my students to stay on task, take care of business first, and remain motivated until the job at hand is complete.

In my first year of teaching, I noticed when we would finish one subject and get ready to begin another, the students would start to talk, move around, hunt for homework, get up to sharpen pencils, and waste a great deal of time trying to get organized. I decided to make subject transitions like a game. I told my students that when they first come to class in the morning, they should organize all their materials so they would be within reach. Then, when we finished with one subject and I would say, "Okay, now let's get out our math books and homework," the kids could put away the materials we had been working with and get out the things needed for math in a matter of seconds.

Sometimes it would get tricky, for example, when I had to use the overhead projector. This required closing the blinds, turning off the lights, closing the door, wheeling out the projector, plugging it in, and pulling down the screen in addition to the students getting out their materials. To accomplish this, I assigned each of the necessary tasks to one student. Then, when I said I needed to use the projector, everyone jumped into action and within a matter of seconds it was ready to go.

Teachers who observe my class always comment on how quickly the kids had the entire room ready for the overhead. Sometimes I would be at the front of the room talking, and a kid might say she couldn't see what I drew on the board. I would say, "Okay, let me show you on the overhead." I would start to walk toward the middle of the room, and before I could get there, the projector had been wheeled there and plugged in, the blinds were closed, lights off, screen down, and pen handed to me. I would casually take the pen and begin to write on the overhead as if it were nothing out of the ordinary. When teachers ask how in the world I got the kids to do it, I tell them that it is easy; kids love to help, they get a kick out of moving from one task to another as quickly as possible, and we practice it over and over again. Before the end of the first month, if you do it correctly, your class will be performing like clockwork.

## RULE 18

*You will make every effort to be as organized as possible.*

Each year, I always ask my former students' new teachers how they are performing in class. Mainly, I am interested in seeing in which areas I had prepared the students well, and the areas where my students have weaknesses. This is sometimes hard to do and very humbling, because it isn't easy hearing a teacher tell you how your students went to her unprepared. If you are really interested in becoming a better teacher, though, I think it is a necessary evaluation. Besides, it is rewarding when you hear positive comments. For example, teachers in the past have said, "I can definitely tell which of my students you taught, because their writing skills are superior to the rest of the class." That is wonderful to hear. But one area where teachers always used to point out weakness in my students, more so than the other students in their classes, was organization. It killed me to hear that, because I thought it must have something to do with the way I was preparing them.

One summer, I was determined to do something that would help make my students become more structured. First, I went shopping and bought a set of the materials I wanted each of my students to have. I found a big ol' binder that would hold their notebooks, loose-leaf paper, pens and pencils, calculator, and calendar. Then I purchased the small, hundred-page notebooks I wanted them to have and other items, like crayons, a ruler, a stapler, etc. I also got a box of tissues, because I found I bought tissues all year because the kids' noses were constantly running.

To keep from having to pay for the tissues myself, I just added a box to their supply list. The next thing I did was place the items out on my living room floor and take a picture of them. I then wrote a letter to the kids explaining the supplies they would need for the year, and I attached the picture to it. They received this three weeks before school began so the parents had plenty of time to find the necessary materials. This was such a good idea. In past years, before I sent out the supply list letter, students walked in on the first day of school equipped with a lot of materials they did not need, and I hated it. The kids, and the parents, too, were usually so excited about the school year that they went ahead and got all of their supply shopping done, even though much of it was for naught. When my students' parents got the picture and letter, they were so appreciative. They weren't rushed to find the supplies, they knew exactly what I wanted them to buy, and they didn't waste any money buying items the kids really didn't need.

On the first day of school, almost all of the students had all the supplies. I found that all parents, regardless of their income, are very supportive of the beginning-of-the-year need for school supplies. In cases where some children didn't show up with the supplies, I had extra sets ready that were supplied by the local church, a car dealership, and a few close friends.

When all the students had their materials on the first day, I was able to go through each item and describe when it was to be used and how they were supposed to label each assignment. I showed them how to keep their homework listed on their calendar pages and where to place papers that had been graded. After walking the class through the system, they became the most organized class I had ever taught, and it made my life a lot easier. When I needed the students to hand in their homework, they all knew where it was. If I needed the kids to get out their review sheets, they went to them immediately. Also, when I had parent-teacher conferences, I was able to go through each child's notebooks and binder with the parents and quickly find any materials, worksheets, or tests I needed. The main thing I learned from that year is that my students enjoyed being organized, and they appreciated the system. After being shown how to be organized, they were able to use that skill not only during that school year but in future years and on into their professional careers.

I recommend that if you are in a profession where you have to instruct others, be as specific as possible about what you expect. If you have to, take pictures and give handouts detailing exactly what you want people to do or produce. Teach them how to be organized by showing examples of how you yourself are organized and the type of structure you expect from them. One thing I have observed is that you should never assume anything about what a student or any person knows or understands how to do. It is always best to be specific about your expectations.

## RULE 19

*When I assign homework, there is to be no moaning or complaining. This will result in a doubled assignment.*

Think about the place where you work. . . . Now think about the people you work with. How many of them would you say are positive people? How many are negative? Which would you rather spend time talking to and working with? I think the answer is obvious, but still, so many people carry negative attitudes and seem to complain about anything they are asked to do or that demands them to put forth effort.

Sometimes there are things we just have to do that we may not want to do at that very moment, but it is our obligation and so we should do it anyway, without moaning or making comments about how we don't want to. Many times, more effort and energy are wasted avoiding something than it would have taken to complete the task. Sometimes when your kids ask you for help on their homework, or when an elderly relative wants you to visit, or the lawn needs mowing, you just don't feel like doing it. That is natural, but it is still an obligation, and it is something that should be done without complaining or giving off a feeling of lethargy.

I try to instill a positive type of attitude in my classroom, and under no circumstances do I allow my students to whine or fuss about any assignments or expectations of them. The punishment I use for this rule, doubling assignments for moaning, however, has given me a lot of grief in the past. Teachers always say, "Mr. Clark, I really don't agree with that Rule 19; you should never use homework as a punishment." I understand their point of view, but at the same time, moaning and complaining about work that is assigned will not be tolerated. To keep it from happening, the consequences for it must be fairly drastic. What do you think is worse: having a class moan about each assignment, spreading the negative feelings about doing the work or having to double the assignment once or twice but having the kids accept each assignment thereafter with no moaning or complaints?

I tell my students that if they do feel the homework is too much for one night, they are welcome to voice their concerns. They must do it in a way that is respectful and stated without whining or complaining. For example, I tell the kids they can state their feelings like this: "Mr. Clark, several of us in the class are performing in a show tonight at the community center. Do you think there is any way you could reduce the number of pages we need to read for homework?" I am always willing to work with kids on issues like that, and I am occasionally open to reducing the amount for the entire class, not for just the ones who have obligations that will keep them from completing all of the work.

## RULE 20

*While you are with a substitute teacher, you will obey the same rules that you follow when I am with you. (I know this is hard, but it is important.)*

We all know what it is like when the boss is away from the office and the workers aren't necessarily in prime production mode. It's the old adage, "When the cat's away, the mice will play." I have seen it in my life when the Dunkin' Donuts manager was out of the store and we would play hide-and-seek or when the principal was away from the school and some teachers would just hand out worksheets and call it a day. I want my students to have the mindset that they are working for themselves and to have pride in their work, whether a boss is standing right over them or not. I want them to be the type of individuals who will give a job 110 percent because they want to and not because they have to.

Instilling that in twelve year olds can be challenging because students can smell a substitute a mile away. They can sense an approaching illness that may cause their teacher to be absent days before any doctor would see it coming. And they can make life miserable for the substitute who is new to them and demonstrates the least amount of fear.

I remember what it was like to be in junior high. I remember the thrill when I saw that lenient substitute walk in the door. I remember once in seventh grade when, while a substitute was in the room, my fellow classmates and I launched an all-out war on one another. The girls used rubber bands that Ginger provided from the supply meant to be used for her braces. The boys picked red berries off Mrs. Gardener's plants that lined the wall next to the windows. There were rubber bands flying here, red berries flying there, and an oblivious substitute teacher sitting at the desk reading a Danielle Steel novel. When Mrs. Gardener walked in the next day, she looked at us, looked at her plants, looked back at us, and said, "What in the hell happened to my berry bushes?" It was not a pretty sight.

To keep my kids from performing as I once did, I use several techniques. The first one is that I talk to the kids a great deal about maintaining order in the classroom even when I am not there. I warn them to be on their best behavior, and I tell them that if I find out anyone was unruly, the consequences will be severe when I return. I love that phrase. "The consequences will be severe." It is great because I am not really saying what I am going to do, so I am not holding myself to anything. Chances are, the whole class could be bad, and I don't want to find myself with thirty-seven kids serving detention for a month. By saying only that it will be "severe," I could really just give them the lecture of their lives and act very disappointed in them and have kept my word.

I have to be honest with you, though. There have been times when the substitutes for my classes have been rude with the students, unreasonable, and not adept at handling a group of students. In those situations, I put almost as much blame on that person for the misbehavior of my students. I never let my students know that; I continue to act angry with them and like the world is coming to an end, but I forgo any consequences. I play the ol' game of, "Oh, you have made me so upset and you are going to regret the consequences," but nothing really comes of it. This is one of my usual statements: "You know, kids, I work hard to provide you with the best education possible, and this is the way you show me your appreciation. Well, I have to tell you, when you do things like this, it makes me not want to follow through with some very neat things I had planned for our class, and that is a shame." That speech works like a charm.

My best technique for getting kids to behave for a substitute actually requires a lot of effort on my part, but it is extremely successful. Sometimes when I know I am going to be absent, I record a video of myself teaching the day's lessons on my iPhone. I will say something like, "Okay, students, now I need for you to get out your novels and turn to page 134. Mrs. Jenkins"—who is the substitute—"if you will please press pause and then press play when all of the students are on the correct page." I then read to the students, stopping to discuss points and clarify items I think they would have questions about. The key to this, however, is a little trick I pull on the kids. First, I tell them at the beginning of the video that I can see each and every one of them in the class, and that if they misbehave, I will know it. Of course, this sounds ridiculous to them, but the day before I'm out I always meet with a couple of students and swear them to secrecy. I tell one kid that when I say I can see the kids in the class, I want him to say, "Mr. Clark, can you really see us?" Then, when the video is playing and the kid asks if I can see the class for real, I reply, "Yes, Berry, I can see you! Now you better pay attention!" It always freaks out the students, and I have even shocked a few substitutes here and there.

There are several reasons I like doing the video. First, the kids don't miss a day of instruction. I am "there" to continue teaching the next day's lesson. Second, I don't have to worry about writing up lesson plans for the substitute. The plans consist of "Press play," then "Press stop." Third, the kids appreciate the effort I take to make the video. They don't always tell me, but when it comes up, I can tell it meant a lot to them that I took the time to make a video for them so that they wouldn't have to do mounds of worksheets and reading. Fourth, discipline is at a minimum. Substitutes comment on how easy it is to control a class when all they have to do is sit back and take the names of kids who aren't paying attention to the video, but they always say that every kid watches the video and pays attention. I act goofy and do neat stunts on the recording, so the kids get into it and really enjoy watching. But please know, I don't record an entire day's lessons. I often just record the first five to ten minutes of each lesson to get the students started and on task.

This idea might also be useful when you are going to be away from your own children while you are on a business trip or on vacation. You can sit down in front of a camera and read one of their favorite storybooks to them. Then, when the child is missing you, he can play the video over and over as many times as he likes. Just because you aren't there doesn't mean you can't be present.

## RULE 21

*We will follow certain classroom protocols. We will be organized, efficient, and on task.*

We have all been in meetings that were disorganized and a waste of time, whether it was the PTA, the town council or a board meeting. Oftentimes there are people who talk too much or there is a lack of leadership and no one to moderate the meeting effectively. When I work with my students, I try to teach them lessons about how to hold yourself in a group, how to debate and discuss issues appropriately, and how to have a conversation within a group.

At RCA there is absolutely no talking by students for the first three days of school. The only way they may speak is if they are answering an adult's question. Those who have seen clips of us dancing on tables and rapping lessons may find it hard to believe our school can be so rigid, but what we learned is that to have fun and a dynamic learning environment you must have structure, rules, and protocols. Once the discipline is in place, anything is possible!

We have learned that when you start strict you can always lighten up; but if you start light, you can never become stricter. When I was teaching in Harlem, the teacher across the hall,

Ms. Higgins, was given what was then called the gifted class. I was given a class of thirty-seven students who were a handful, and I was prepared to teach my fifty-five rules on day one! I encouraged Ms. Higgins, a first-year teacher, to do the same, but she replied that she didn't want to seem so strict and that she would see how the first few days went. Well, on day three my class was a disaster. Kids were loud, disorderly, and a mess. Her class, however, was perfect. Absolutely perfect. She told me that she wouldn't be using my rules and that her kids were a really great and well-behaved bunch. I begged her and explained that all students are the absolute best they are going to be during the first week of school and that she needed to use that time to put structure and procedures in place. She wouldn't budge.

Jump ahead to October 1st. I had been consistent and diligent with the enforcement of my fifty-five rules, and my class was the most impressive thing you have ever seen. From the way they walked down the hall, addressed adults, sat upright in their chairs, clapped for each other, and kept the bathroom spotless—they were on point! Ms. Higgins's class, however, was in crisis. The principal met with her and had the "You have to get control of your class" talk. She came to me and asked me to help her implement my rules; I tried to help, but by then all was lost. If you start soft, you can't become stricter. If you do, the students will think you are mean. If you start strict they will just assume that is the way it is and they will fall in line. On November 1st, Ms. Higgins quit, and we lost someone who could have been an exceptional teacher.

If you can start from day one and obtain control over a class, you can do some really neat projects. There have been times when we have done group projects and used glue, ribbons, balloons, and just about anything you can think of, but the kids remained focused and organized. I call it "organized chaos." We are able to do group work and have a lot of fun, but it is orderly and we get much more accomplished. If you don't have that structure in the classroom and you try to do hands-on cooperative learning, you are going to have a zoo.

Another protocol I put into place is how to answer questions in class. I used to ask students for their opinions during lessons, and as they responded I assumed the entire class was listening. They sure looked like they were listening. It wasn't until I started asking this question, "Can any of you tell me what she just said?" that I realized no one was. The students would just respond with blank faces of "Whaaaat?" I learned that as a teacher when you ask a child a question, you and the child are engaged. Most likely, most of the rest of the class isn't. They see it as a time to daydream. I put a few rules in place to combat this. I had the students start to stand to deliver their opinions and ideas. They were told to completely turn their feet toward the rest of the class (that is important) and to look students in the eye as they explain their thoughts. Sometimes they will even tell the students, "Lean in," to make sure the group is following along. When the student is finished, other students are allowed to comment as well, and they don't have to raise their hands. They just simply stand and then speak. If two speak at the same time, one needs to say, "Oh, after you," and the other one will state his or her opinion. When finished, the child will "throw it back" to the other student by saying, "That is how I feel about the issue, but I believe James had a point he wanted to share as well."

The intent is to remove me from the situation and turn the class into a living organism where the students are talking and having an in-depth dialogue without me acting as the moderator. The students are encouraged to use connecting phrases like, "I really appreciate your idea, but," and, "I respectfully disagree with your statement because..." Students are also encouraged to notice who isn't speaking and to pull them into the discussion by saying things like, "That is how I feel, but I am really interested in hearing your opinion, Sara."

When people visit RCA, they say the students carry on conversations better than adults in corporate America. It isn't that our ten year olds are smarter than those adults, it's just that they have been given the tools and protocols for how to conduct themselves in an appropriate manner. With guidance and specific examples, all children, and in fact all people, perform at higher levels and have a greater chance of achieving success. They just need to be specifically shown the way.

## RULE 22

*Go out of your way to make others feel special. "See people."*

Throughout my life I have noticed that people who tend to be successful have a way of making people feel special. It's an ability to look others in the eyes and make individuals feel as if they are, in that moment, the most important person in the world.

My family never had money while I was growing up, and my parents may not have been successful in the conventional sense, but in our small town they were successful because of the way they treated people. When we would go to the Piggly Wiggly grocery store, it would take forever to finish our shopping because everyone wanted to come up and talk to my mom and dad. "Oh, Jean! It's so good to see you," they would say. My mom would smile and listen and show so much love to everyone. She would ask about their family members, their pets, their health. She just had a way of making people feel important. My dad would joke with people, look them right in the eye, and give them his full attention. "Ronnie Clark, you old son of a gun," they would say. We'd be there so long I would say, "Mom, Dad, this carton of milk done got hot. Want me to swap it for a fresh one?"

Once I had the honor of eating dinner with Oprah Winfrey. There were a lot of people at the table and I was four seats down from her, but, trust me, I was watching her the whole time! Whenever waitstaff approached the table, she would take their hands and say, "You are doing such a good job of taking care of us all. These people mean a lot to me and you are doing a wonderful job." Of course, they were already trying their hardest because it was Oprah Winfrey's table, but when she spoke to them in that manner, it was like lightning flew through them. They would respond, "Yes ma'am," and then take off, working even harder to meet the needs of the table.

When I first got to the school in Harlem, there was a fight between two young boys. The resource officer took one of the boys and sat him in the office, and then the officer went to call his mom and get the principal. The boy was sitting there, huffing and puffing with wild abandon, and I didn't know what to do. I eventually just sat down beside him and he continued to clench his fists and huff to no end. I finally leaned over to him and whispered, "I was breathing like that one time, and I passed out." After two seconds, the huffing stopped, he turned directly to me and asked, "For real?"

In that moment, I tried to channel my parents. I looked right at him and tried to make him feel as if the world had washed away. I asked him to tell me about his day from the moment he woke up until that instant. He soon was calm and explaining the situation. Then he said, "You're different. If you were my teacher I don't think I would get in any trouble." I eventually taught that child, and he sure did still get in trouble, but it was manageable. I think it was manageable because my interactions with him were led from compassion. I focused on him and his well-being above all else.

I try to continue to use this strategy at RCA. When students stop me in the hall, I turn to face them and seem to let the world fall away. I'll say, "Do you need to talk about something? I've got time." Honestly, I never have time, but when you are dealing with children, you make time. When I walk through the lobby, I hug the parents and say, "I am so glad to be on a team with you! You are an incredible mom and with both of us working together, there is no way your child isn't going to be successful." I make a point to learn the names of my staff's pets. I ask about loved one's colonoscopies. I try to be someone who "sees" people with a true desire to connect with and uplift them, and I try to encourage my students to do the same.

There are three key things I ask them to do:

1. See the situation from another perspective. How might that individual feel? What life experiences could be affecting their decisions? What could be their point of motivation?

2. Have empathy for others. Realize that when others are difficult or hard to get along with, there can be hurt, emotional scarring or negative past experiences that contribute to their behavior. In those moments, instead of getting angry because you don't understand their actions, feel empathy for them and seek to understand their motivations. Understand that the world isn't rosy for everyone, and show compassion for all with whom you interact.

3. Never rush an interaction. People know if you are blowing them off. You may be in a hurry, but for the moments you do interact with someone, relax, be calm, look people in the eye, and "see" them. Then, when you apologize for having to go, it will seem genuine because it isn't rushed or sporadic.

## RULE 23

*Quickly learn the names of other teachers in the school and greet them by saying things like, "Good morning, Mrs. Graham" or, "Good afternoon, Ms. Ortiz. That is a very pretty dress." (Note: If you are in line with the rest of the class, you are not allowed to speak to the teachers at that time because the no-talking rule is in effect. You should speak to other teachers if you are entering or leaving school, at recess, on an errand or changing classes.)*

It always surprises me when I talk to people who don't know the names of their neighbors or who can't name all of their immediate coworkers. It is a shame that people don't go out of their way to introduce themselves more often, especially when there is someone new in the workplace or in the neighborhood/community. I hope that as my students go through life they will learn to get to know the people who live and work around them and try to make people who are just starting out at their job or where they live feel comfortable and welcomed in their new surroundings. I want them to get used to learning the names of those around them and to make an effort to be kind and polite to everyone. I think this makes for a more comfortable and enjoyable place to live and work, and they will be far happier in those environments.

When I went to P.S. 83 in Harlem, I felt that trust and comfortable feeling was established to a point. The assistant principal, Mrs. Castillo, was an outstanding individual who acted as the mother figure of teachers and students alike. She knew the name of every child and was respected by all. There were also teachers who had been there for four or five years whom the students respected and loved. On the other hand, there were a number of new faces in the school each year. My first week at the school, there were more than ten new teachers. Of the initial group, after a couple of weeks, five left and five more were added. Of those new five, three left and were replaced by new ones, all before Christmas. This made it hard for bonds to be made that would unify the entire school. To help matters, I asked the kids to learn the names of all of the teachers in the school to help create that unified atmosphere. I feel that if the kids know everyone in the school, they are more comfortable in the school. The more adults in the school they know, the more people there are for them to turn to when they have problems or need help.

In addition, as a teacher, it is nice when the students know who you are and speak to you. Imagine a new teacher walking into a school for the first time. He or she is probably nervous about entering the new environment and worried the kids won't like him or her. In most schools, teachers have activities to welcome new faculty members, but I think it can be more effective if the students give a positive welcome as well.

## RULE 24

*Flush the toilet and wash your hands after using the restroom. When in a public restroom, get a paper towel before washing your hands. After washing your hands, use the paper towel to turn off the faucets and to press the dispenser to get another paper towel to dry your hands. (Or use the towel to press the*

*button to start the dryer.) The last thing you want to
do is touch areas with clean hands that others have
touched with dirty hands.*

All I am really asking is that people take cleanliness into
account when they're using a public restroom. We all know
that bathroom facilities can sometimes make that a very hard
thing to do. It drives me crazy when there is no soap in those
little dispensers. And just what is going on with those sen-
sored faucets that only run water for about one and a half seconds? I find myself waving my hands under the faucet to get it
to begin, but by the time I get both hands under the water, it
has shut off. It makes washing your hands a chore.

Those difficulties aside, public restrooms can be a nightmare. From unflushed toilets to floors littered with tissue, it
can be a pretty unsanitary and disgusting experience.

My first year of teaching, I kept noticing how the urinals
in the boys' restroom were never flushed. It drove me crazy!
I asked the kids why they never flushed the toilet and I got
two responses: 1. I don't want to touch the handle because it's
nasty, and 2. We don't flush at home unless it is a number two
because it wastes water and costs money.

To solve the first problem, I told the kids to get a paper
towel after they finished using the restroom and use the paper
towel to touch the handle. For the second one, I asked how
many of them liked to use a toilet that had someone else's
urine in it. No one did, of course, and so I reinforced the need
to take care of your own business and not to leave it there
for others to deal with. Thankfully, the kids took what I said
to heart and there were clean bowls from then on. The kids

in my class even started to remind other kids to flush if they were just going to walk away.

The second problem is that kids take their dirty hands and turn on the faucet, then they wash their hands, and then they turn off the faucet where they had just placed their dirty hands. To solve that problem, I ask the kids to get a paper towel before washing their hands. I tell them to use that towel to turn off the faucet after washing their hands and to then use it to dispense another paper towel. (I know this may seem neurotic, but when you are a schoolteacher and you come in contact with every germ known to humanity, you learn that if you want to survive, you have to stop the germs where they start!)

In terms of overall bathroom cleanliness, I talk to the students a lot about how hard the custodians work and how it is easy for us to help them by doing a few very small things. The first is making sure that there are no paper towels left on the bathroom floor. This is nearly impossible because teenage boys think they are Stephen Curry, and they're not. Missed baskets always line the floor around the trash can. I make a point to tell the boys, and the girls as well, to take a paper towel and go around the entire bathroom and pick up any trash left on the floor and dispose of it. I make sure to tell them I don't care if they put the trash on the floor or not, but what matters is that the floor is clean when they leave. It has made a huge difference in the look of the room, and the kids take pride in that.

## RULE 25

*We will often have visitors to our school. If someone is visiting our class, I send two students to the front door of the building with a sign welcoming the person. When our visitor arrives, shake hands, tell them who you are, and welcome the person to our school. Then take the visitor on a small tour of the building before bringing them to the classroom.*

This technique can be used whether you are having visitors come to your office or you are having a guest at a party who doesn't know anyone other than you. It is all about making the person feel comfortable and welcome in their new surroundings. For the visiting businessperson, have him greeted at the door and given a brief tour of your office. Have him taken personally to your office and introduced to you. For the party guest, have another friend of yours meet him at the door and take him around the party, introducing him to your other guests.

Entering an unknown environment can be intimidating and scary. When I was a sophomore in high school, my parents moved within North Carolina from Chocowinity to Belhaven, and I had to go to a new high school where I knew no one. On that first day I was terrified. My parents told me that the school would assign me a buddy to show me around, but that never happened. I was all alone, and going from class to class was bad enough, but I most dreaded lunchtime because I knew I would be eating alone. Luckily, during fourth period

I was assigned a lab partner, Anita. She turned to me and said, "You must be new, so you're going to eat lunch with my friends and me and I won't take no for an answer." She didn't have to worry about that; I was so relieved. I ended up becoming best friends with Anita and her friends, and I grew to love that school. I never forgot, however, the awkward feeling on the first day of not knowing anyone or where to go or what to expect.

I want to make sure everyone who visits feels welcome. Walking into a school can be especially intimidating when you don't know where to go or who you need to speak with. To manage this situation, I have two students wait at the front door with a welcome sign that has the visitor's name written clearly. This is carefully timed so that little instruction time is missed. When the guest arrives, I have the students greet her and conduct a small tour of the school. They then escort her to the room and introduce her to the class. This process takes a lot of practice, and I usually have a group of kids stay after school one day to practice giving the tour. We go over introductions, information they should give, and questions they should ask. This is a respectful gesture appreciated by everyone who visits the school.

## RULE 26

*Do not save seats in the lunchroom. If someone wants to sit down, let them. Do not try to exclude anyone. We are a family, and we must treat one another with respect and kindness.*

We have all felt left out at some time or another, often at the mercy of other adults. When kids in the classroom are the ones being excluded, it can be a nightmare for any teacher. I hate to see kids who are isolated and left alone. I start from day one talking to the students about being a family and including one another. I tell them to be a friend to everyone in the class and not just a select few. I also tell them, however, that they don't have to like everyone in the class. I tell them that, as an adult, I don't like every adult I meet. I tell them it is only human not to like everyone, but I make sure to try to treat each person with kindness and respect regardless of my feelings. I inform them that I expect the same type of behavior from them as well.

If I notice at lunchtime that kids are sitting in the same seats every day or seats are being saved, I give the kids a warning. If it happens again, I utilize a seating chart. I make sure to seat students in a way so that everyone has someone to talk to and no one is left out. I usually tell them they have to sit like that until I say otherwise. (I love that phrase, "until I say otherwise." It is often not a good idea to put an amount of time on a punishment, because you never know what may happen to cause you to want to lessen or lengthen it.)

It takes a while for students to learn to accept everyone because there is a certain amount of safety in being part of a clique. Even as adults, we want a sense of belonging, and unfortunately the bonding of some means the exclusion of others. It's okay to have groups of friends, but I teach my students that it is important to make sure they and their friends accept others and include others in their activities.

# RULE 27

*If I or any other teacher in the school is speaking to or disciplining a student, do not look at that student. You wouldn't want others looking at you if you were in trouble or being reprimanded, so don't look at others in that situation. If you are the student I am talking to, do not get angry or fuss at students who are looking at you. Let me know and I will handle the situation.*

Julia Jones is the sole origin of this rule. Julia was consistently in trouble. You name it, she did it. Whenever I would try to reprimand her, matters would only escalate when other students watched as she was scolded. She would lash out at them, verbally or physically, and become extremely hostile. I had to keep that from happening at all costs, so I told all of the students that if I was disciplining another student, they were not to look. They were to keep their heads down or facing forward. This rule worked like a charm, not only with Julia, but with all of the students.

Imagine being pulled over for speeding. The cop asks you to get out of the car. As you are talking to him, every passerby turns to stare at you. It's not a good feeling, and in fact, it makes matters worse. My co-teacher from North Carolina, Barbara Jones, always said her greatest fear was that she was going to be pulled over by a cop and that every school bus was going to pass by with all of her students waving and pointing out the windows. It is one thing to be punished, and another to be in trouble and have everyone know about it and watch as you are scolded.

In school, kids are inevitably going to get into trouble and there will be times when they must be reprimanded. To avoid the embarrassment and the anger a public spectacle can create, I make sure the kids know and understand this rule. I also make sure the kids understand that if a student stares at someone I am talking sternly to, the student who is staring will be punished as well.

## RULE 28

*If you have a question about your homework, you may call or text me. If I am not able to answer the phone, please leave a message in the following manner: "Hi, Mr. Clark, this is_____. I need help with the homework. You can call me back until ?:00. Thank you." Leave this message once; there is no need to leave this message fourteen times.*

I have no problem whatsoever giving students my phone number, although many teachers do not give out theirs. I don't blame them; it could turn into a nightmare if your phone is constantly ringing. However, it really isn't that bad, because most students don't call often, but I think it makes them feel good to know that they can call me if they need to. It gives them a type of security, and it shows them I care enough to share my personal time with them if they need me.

I do explain to my students what an appropriate call is. I tell them that calling me to find out what their homework is isn't acceptable. They should have made sure to copy it down in class, and if they didn't copy it down, they need to call a fellow student. If they call me, I will tell them the assignment, but they will have silent lunch and lose their recess on the next school day. A call that is appropriate is about problems with the homework. Oftentimes in a class of over thirty students, it is hard to give individual attention to the ones who need it. Also, many kids are embarrassed to admit in front of other students that they need help. Giving my phone number to them gives those kids an opportunity to get individual attention from me that isn't possible in school. In Harlem, there was a girl named Maria who was very quiet and shy in the classroom. She never raised her hand or let on that she was confused. Each night, however, she would call me and we would speak for about five minutes about the night's assignment. She often just needed more clarification and a little help getting started. For Maria, that made all the difference in her school year, and not only academically. She knew she wasn't alone and that she had me to support her and help her.

For teachers who are worried their phones may ring constantly, I rarely have more than two calls a day. It is important to give my number, though, because no child can walk in my class and claim they didn't do their homework because they didn't understand it. I take away that excuse, because they could have called me.

## RULE 29

*There are several manners dealing with food that you must follow: I call these my ABCs of etiquette.*

A.  When you first sit down for a meal, immediately place your napkin in your lap. If your silverware is wrapped in a napkin, unwrap it as soon as you sit down and place the napkin in your lap.

B.  When finished eating, place your napkin on the table to the left of your plate. Place it loosely beside the plate. Don't crumple it, because you don't want to seem untidy. Don't fold it too neatly, because you don't want the restaurant to think you are going to use it again. If you leave the table during the meal, it is appropriate to leave your napkin on the seat of your chair. Never place your napkin on the table until the meal is complete.

C.  Never place your elbows on the table.

D.  Use one hand to eat, unless you are cutting or buttering food. Never have your fork in one hand and a glass in the other.

E.  Do not lick your fingers. There is a napkin provided for the purpose of cleaning your fingers. There is no need to lick yourself clean.

F.  Do not smack your lips and chew noisily.

G.  Do not chew with your mouth open.

H.  Do not talk with your mouth full. Sometimes people will place a hand over their mouth and talk anyway.

Don't do that. Wait until you have swallowed your food to speak.

I. If something is caught in your teeth, don't go in after it; wait until you are in the restroom to remove it.

J. Do not slurp.

K. Do not play with your food.

L. If you drop your fork, napkin or anything else on the floor, do not pick it up. It is very rude and unsanitary to place something on the table that has been on the floor. If you pick up something that has dropped and hand it to a waiter, then you will need to excuse yourself and wash your hands before continuing with your meal. The best way to handle a situation when something has dropped on the floor is to ask a waiter for a replacement; leave the old one on the floor.

M. You are to use your utensils for eating almost everything. Here are ten types of foods you may use your hands to eat:

    a. Pizza

    b. Bacon

    c. Cookies

    d. Bread (Always tear off a bite-sized piece to eat. If you are going to use butter, never butter the whole piece of bread; butter the piece you tore off, and eat that before tearing another piece.)

    e. Corn on the cob (It is appropriate to eat across instead of eating around.)

    f. Hot dogs, hamburgers, and sandwiches (including breakfast biscuits)

g. French fries and chips

h. Fried chicken

i. Small vegetables like carrots or celery

j. Small fruits like grapes on a stem, apples, oranges, etc.

N. Never reach over someone's plate to get something. You should say, "Will you please pass the salt?"

O. Never start eating off of your tray until you have reached the table and are seated.

P. When we are eating at a restaurant, do not begin eating until everyone at the table has received their food. If you receive your meal first, you must sit patiently. If you didn't receive your food but others did, you may choose to say, "Please, feel free to go ahead and enjoy your meal." If you already have your food you must respond, "Oh no, it's okay. I don't mind waiting." At that point the person without their meal should reply, "I insist." And at that, you may begin eating. You should never begin unless you have been prompted twice to eat!

Q. Never complain if the line is too long, the food isn't good or if there is a wait. You don't want to be negative to the point where you spoil the enjoyment of the event for others.

R. If you are unsure which silverware to use, simply start with the fork, knife or spoon that is the farthest from your plate. On the left, you will have your salad fork on the outside and your dinner fork on the inside. On the far right, you will have your soup spoon. Beside it you will have the spoon you will use to stir your coffee or tea, then your salad knife, and then your dinner knife. The utensils above your plate are to be used for dessert.

S.  When finished eating, do not push your plate away from you. Leave it where it is in the setting. To show you have finished eating, lay your fork and knife together diagonally across the plate. You should place the fork with the tines down, and you should have the sharp side of the knife facing you. Of the two utensils, the fork should be closest to you.

T.  Never place a piece of silverware that you have used back on the table. Leave it on a plate or saucer.

U.  If you didn't use a utensil, do not place it on a plate or saucer when you are finished. Just leave it where it is.

V.  Always look the server in the eye when you are ordering, asking a question or saying thank you.

W.  Make a point to remember the server's name when he or she introduces themself to you. Use their name as often as possible throughout the course of the meal.

X.  If you have to go to the restroom, you should stand up and say, "Excuse me," as you leave the table.

Y.  When you are offered desserts or asked a question such as, "What sides would you like?" or, "What dressing would you like for your salad?" it is best to be prepared. Check the menu thoroughly so that you know the available options. Additionally, if you are ordering meat, as you place your order, mention if you would like the food to be prepared well-done, medium-well, medium, medium-rare or rare.

Z.  Never talk to waitstaff as if they are servants. Treat them with respect and kindness, and remember, they are the ones who are fixing your food and bringing it to you. You do not want to be on the bad side of the waitstaff.

I realize expecting kids to abide by these rules may seem a bit much, but actually I have found that the kids really enjoy learning the manners and putting them into practice. It is always a shock to people when they walk into the lunchroom and see my kids eating with their napkins in their laps, eating with one hand, and using perfect table manners. In "Cafeteria World" that is almost an anomaly.

I remember when I was in junior high and my family and I were at my cousin Sheila's wedding. At the very fancy reception, everyone sat quietly in front of the elaborate place settings, not knowing one another and struggling to make conversation. In the center of the table was a dish containing little pieces of something in the shape of flowers. After about two minutes where no one at the table said a word, my mother, bless her heart, in an attempt to ease the tension, reached for one of the pieces, saying, "Look, Ron, would you like a mint?" As she picked up the flower, it smashed between her fingers. She then realized it was not a mint but butter, and in her embarrassment she turned three shades of red. Then she started to laugh at herself. Soon the entire table was laughing and we ended up having a wonderful night of conversation and laughter.

Even though that situation turned out well, I don't want my students to end up in a position like my mother or me, feeling uncomfortable, not knowing what to do or how to handle themselves. If the kids ever need to eat at a formal dinner, there would be no reason for them to feel they aren't prepared to go or that they would be embarrassed.

# RULE 30

*After we eat, we clean up after ourselves. This includes cleaning off the tables and making sure we haven't left any trash on the floor or around the eating area. It is important to be responsible for your trash no matter where you are and to not litter.*

As a general rule, kids are messy eaters. Visit a lunchroom, and you will likely see napkins littering the floor, remains of spilled food, and lunch tables askew. That really bothers me because if kids are allowed to get away with that in school, then they are going to carry that behavior with them when they are at McDonald's or any other restaurant or eating establishment. I make sure that when my students leave their tables, we leave them exactly as we found them. We pick up all of the trash, wipe the tables clean, and make sure there is no stray paper around the trash cans. In the beginning I have to remind them every day, but after I work with them for a couple of months, they know to pick up their trash before they leave. By the end of the year, there isn't any trash on the floor to pick up. They have learned that instead of having to clean up after themselves, they can be more careful as they eat and there will be no mess to worry about.

I have always been annoyed by littering of any kind, not only in food establishments. I stress to the kids to take pride in their school and community. They should not only refrain from littering, but they should also pick up trash that has been left by others. I often do small tests with kids to see if they are adhering to that rule. I will place a few pieces of trash around the room before the students arrive, and then I will see who picks them up. After everyone is seated, I will tell them that the ones who picked up the trash will get free ice cream at lunch. I always point out the kids who glanced at the trash but walked past it without picking it up. Believe me when I tell you that there will not be a piece of trash left on that floor for weeks after a trick like that.

One day I was reminding my students about not littering, and a boy named Pablo said, "Mr. Clark, the other day I was hanging out at the convenience store with my friends and we saw a sign they have up in there that says 'No Littering,' so they must be serious about keeping trash off the floor, too." I thought it was interesting that there was a sign inside the store that said no littering, so the next time I was there I looked for it. Sure enough, there was a sign, but it actually read, "No Loitering." I thought of Pablo standing there with his friends, hanging out, making sure not to litter, but all the while they were doing the opposite of what the sign was asking.

The point, though, is that kids become aware of the importance of keeping areas clean and taking ownership of their own trash. I am always so proud of my students by the end of the year and the way they become conscious of their own actions and gain respect for their school and community and make sincere efforts to keep them clean.

# RULE 31

*When we stay in a hotel room, it is appropriate to leave a tip on the pillow for the hotel workers who are responsible for cleaning the room after our stay. Two to three dollars per night is an appropriate amount, depending on the cost of the room.*

I have found that most students know they are supposed to tip a waiter or taxi driver, but most haven't heard they are supposed to tip housekeeping in their hotel room as well. I recently was on a trip with my college roommates, and one left $12 on the dresser before he left the room. I asked him why he was leaving such a large tip, and he told me that his mother works in a hotel and she always complains that most people don't leave any tip and that many who do just leave the change out of their pockets. He said he always tips extra to make up for the many rooms where there is no tip at all. That just emphasized to me the importance of leaving some amount to show appreciation for having the room cleaned. I hope that by enforcing that gesture in my students now, it will have an impact on them and remain a practice they continue for the rest of their lives. When we are on trips, I don't expect the students to leave their own spending money as a tip. For all of our trips, we have fund-raisers to pay for the entire trip, and the tip money is included as part of the budget.

I know some people may not be accustomed to leaving tips in hotel rooms because essentially they are leaving money for someone they never see or have any contact with. Doing things for someone who can never thank you personally is the message of the saying, "What goes around, comes around." You should be kind to everyone and show appreciation to those who do things for you, and in return it can bring only good things for you. Speaking of leaving tips, I think no one can appreciate how important it is to leave an appropriate tip unless you have worked for tips yourself. I guarantee that if you are waiting tables you will not find a better tipper than someone who has also waited tables.

## RULE 32

*When we ride on a bus, van, or plane, we will always sit facing forward. We never turn around to talk to other students, stick anything into the aisles, stick our faces between the seats or misbehave. When we exit, we always say thank you and wish the driver, conductor or crew a good day.*

Field trips can be nerve-racking! I have taken students everywhere from New York City to Utah to South Africa to China, and I have learned that the behavior you expect from students is the behavior you will get. If you don't prepare them accordingly, it can be a catastrophe. It is hard enough to drive a large vehicle, but then you have the added pressure of having the lives of so many students in your hands. The last thing a driver or crew needs is thirty screaming kids as a distraction.

I have seen and heard nightmare stories about kids who

throw things out of bus windows and break other vehicles' windshields. I have heard of students who were fighting on the bus but the driver was too scared to get involved so he didn't even bother stopping. There are times when objects are actually thrown at drivers, and kids who try to make them swerve and drive off the road. I know of one teacher's daughter who was dared to moon a car out of the back window of the bus; she did, and the driver of that car turned out to be the superintendent. Oh me!

I have seen school groups that basically played musical chairs the entire flight. They were loud, obnoxious, and rude to the flight attendants. In those situations, the chaperones usually try to sleep and ignore the chaos. I always feel so bad for the other passengers whose flight has been made miserable. Whether it's my students or my relatives, I don't like to see any child cause so much unnecessary stress on others, and therefore we practice how to ride on various types of transportation.

Prior to a trip, I set the chairs in my classroom up as if it is a bus, van or airplane. We practice getting on the transport, and the students have to look at the driver or flight attendant and greet them with a big smile. They then have to practice walking down the aisle taking note that their backpack or luggage doesn't touch anyone or any of the chairs. When they get to their seat, they have to enter the aisle without touching the back of the seat in front of them. (Many people pull on that seat for balance, but it is a bother to the person actually sitting there.) For flights, they are told never to pull down the tray, because the flight attendant will have to ask them to raise it before takeoff. If they listen to headphones, they must select the desired volume and then hold the earbuds in front of them. If they can hear the music, they must turn it down until it is no longer audible; at that point, they can place them in their ears. When the flight attendant offers a drink, they are instructed to say, "May I please have a _____?" They are never to ask for seconds. If they have to use the restroom, they are told to say, "Excuse me," to others who may have to move and be inconvenienced. If there is a game console on the seat in front of them, they are asked to be mindful to press lightly so that the person in front of them isn't bothered. While talking, nothing above a whisper is permissible and they are not allowed to talk between or across the aisle. Upon exiting the flight, they should always thank the flight attendants for a wonderful flight. And lastly, if they are presented with wings or other gifts from the crew, they should act like they were given $1,000 and show appropriate appreciation. (I have had kids look at the metal wings like, "What am I supposed to do with this?" so covering that ahead of time is important.)

Traveling with kids is stressful, and there will always be hiccups, but if you can spell out and role-play your expectations ahead of time, you will end up with fewer headaches in the long run.

## RULE 33

*When we go on field trips, we will meet different people. When I introduce you, make sure you remember their names. Then, when we are leaving,*

*make sure to shake their hands and thank them,*
*mentioning their names as you do so.*

The first year my class was invited to the White House, the president and Mrs. Clinton took the time to shake the hands of each student and parent. I noticed Mrs. Clinton did a very good job of remembering each student's name, and as we were leaving and she was telling the students goodbye, she called each child by name. I was really impressed by that, but it didn't end there. Two years later, I was at the White House with a different group of students and again we talked to Mrs. Clinton. Not only did she once again do a great job remembering each child's name quickly, she also asked me how one of my former students, Marus, was doing, and she asked about him by name! Now, I am sure part of this is due to the fact that Mrs. Clinton has an incredible memory, but I also noticed something else that she does. When she is introduced to someone, she always replies to them and ends her statement by saying their name. This reinforces in her memory the name of the person. I started to teach my kids to do the same thing, and we practiced like this:

**Mr. Clark:** "Students, I would like to introduce you to Mr. Wallace, the owner of this theater."

**Student:** "It is a pleasure to meet you, Mr. Wallace. Thank you so much for giving us this tour of your theater."

Then, upon leaving:

Student:     "Again, Mr. Wallace, on behalf of my fellow stu-
             dents I would like to thank you for the hospital-
             ity that you have shown us today. We have all
             learned a great deal about how theaters work
             and the role they play in the movie industry.
             Thank you again."

We role-play situations like that quite a bit to give the students adequate practice.

People respect you more when you refer to them by their
name; and not remembering someone's name can cause an
awkward moment. This rule is all about avoiding that situation and using the person's name as quickly as you can after
learning it so you won't forget it.

As a side note to Rule 33: If we are on a field trip and
I introduce you to someone while you are sitting down, you
must stand up to shake the person's hand. It is very rude to
remain seated when being introduced to someone.

## RULE 34

*Whenever you are offered food, whether it be on a
buffet or treats in class, never take more than your
fair share. You never want to be greedy and try to get
more than you should, not only because it is waste-
ful, but also because it is disrespectful to others when
you do not leave enough for them.*

The first time I took my students to a buffet, I was shocked at how much food they piled on their plates.

We were at a pizzeria, and students were coming back to the table with five or six slices each. Since then I have set limits on how much the students can place on their plates. I tell them they cannot cover more than three-quarters of the plate and that they cannot pile anything on top of something else. When kids are hungry, though, this rule can be hard to enforce.

When we were at Disney's American Teacher Awards and I walked to the podium to give my acceptance speech, I took four of my students onstage with me. I was thrilled to win for many reasons, and one of them is quite funny. I was excited that I won because I have always wondered where the winners go on award shows when they walk offstage. I used to wonder, "Who is back there, and just what are they doing?" Well, when the kids and I got to go backstage, I was glad to finally find out. There were reporters on one side for interviews, a large-screen TV showing what was going on with the show, and a replica of the onstage podium where we stood to have our pictures taken. There was also a buffet, and my students were allowed to fix small plates as I was interviewed.

Suddenly, a lady came up to me and said that we had to make it back to our table quickly because the next award was about to be presented. As I called the kids over and told them we had to hurry back, I was stunned to see that one of my students, Sabrina, had piled nine hot wings on her plate. I said, "Sabrina, I can't believe you! Don't you remember that Rule 34 is about gluttony!" She replied that she was hungry, but I told her we didn't have time to eat because we had to hurry back to our table, and I told her to dump the plate in the trash. She did so, and we began to make our way back to our seats. As we meandered our way through table after table, passing guests such as Oprah Winfrey and former Disney CEO Michael Eisner, I smiled and nodded my head in greeting. I glanced back to see three of my students, Brad, David, and Trevor, following me and doing the same very gracefully, but then I noticed Sabrina pulling up the rear, smiling at first, but then trying to discreetly take a bite of one of the chicken wings she was still holding!

Even though the enforcement of Rule 34 doesn't always work that well, kids usually get the idea and do really well with not being gluttonous. Sometimes when I pass out Rice Krispies treats or brownies to the students, there will be individuals who will glance over them, trying to find the biggest one for themselves. If I notice students doing that, I skip them and wait until everyone else has selected theirs before giving them a chance. The same applies when we have pizza parties; there will always be kids looking for the biggest slice of pizza, and it just takes constant reinforcement to remind the kids that they aren't the only ones who are hungry and who want the big piece of pizza. It takes a while to teach them to sacrifice their desire for the biggest piece in order to be respectful to others and not to assume they deserve to have the biggest amount.

After explaining why it's more polite to take a small amount, I always reward the students who try to put this into practice. For example, if I see a kid purposely take the smallest piece of pizza or brownie, I will go back to them after everyone else has gotten one and offer them an extra piece because their first one was so small. That reinforcement works well, and after a while the majority of the class begins to put others before themselves.

## RULE 35

*Whether we are in school or on a field trip, if someone drops something, pick it up and hand it back to them. Even if they are closer to the object, it is only polite to make the gesture of bending down to retrieve the item.*

Recently, I was walking across a parking lot, and my bank card and license fell out of my pocket. Before I could bend down, a little boy who was about ten feet away from me ran over and picked up the cards and handed them back to me. I was so surprised and pleased. I thanked him loudly and looked around for his mother. She was watching him the entire time. She definitely looked like a lady who had her act together, and I am sure his good manners came from her instruction and guidance.

In the classroom, it used to drive me crazy when a student's pencil would roll off of a desk and no one would pick it up. The kid would have to get up and walk around to get the pencil. Everyone else would just ignore it. After pointing out to kids how I expected them to pick up anything someone else dropped, they did it, and didn't have a problem with it.

After a while, it really became commonplace to them. Once, we were on a field trip to see a play in Times Square and a lady who was finished with her pack of cigarettes just threw it on the ground. One of the little girls in the class, Jocelyn, ran and picked it up and chased down the woman saying, "Ma'am, you dropped this!" The woman looked at Jocelyn like she was crazy and put the empty pack back in her pocket. Well, picking up someone else's trash isn't exactly what I intended, but hey, it sent an important message to that lady nonetheless.

## RULE 36

*If you approach a door and someone is following you, hold the door. If the door opens by pulling, pull it open, stand to the side, and allow the other person to pass through first. Then you can walk through. If the door opens by pushing, hold the door after you pass through.*

After seeing kids try to cram through doors in the school and watching them enter restaurants as the door slammed on other customers, I knew I had to address this issue with my students. Teaching them small acts of kindness, such as letting someone else go through a door first as they hold it open, may seem insignificant, but it can go a long way toward helping students realize how to respect and appreciate others. I always have the second person in line hold the door, and have the other students say, "Thank you," as they walk through.

Hearing appreciation so many times is a great way to reiterate the importance of doing the right thing.

Additionally, when I told my students that they should say, "Excuse me," when someone bumps into them, they responded, "What if it wasn't my fault?" I explained that saying, "Excuse me," is the way to handle the situation whether it was their fault or not and that they could also add, "After you," as they allow the other person to go first. To that, the students retorted, "What if I want to go first?" I had to explain that sometimes allowing others to go first allows them to really be first, because they are showing they are more mature. I actually practice this with the students in the hallway so that they can work on showing the appropriate body language and hand gestures.

If we don't point out these things to kids, most of them aren't going to figure them out on their own. Even with such a simple and basic rule as holding the door for others or saying excuse me, I am always shocked at how many questions my students have about it, and they are anxious to learn exactly what they are supposed to do. I find that is the case for almost all of these rules; the kids want to know just what is expected of them and how to show respect. Once they've been told, they're halfway there.

## RULE 37

*Be a good listener.*

Being a good listener isn't something that comes naturally to people, and for most children it needs to be taught. When we first start practicing with students, it almost appears as if they are going to crawl out of their skin because they don't have a phone in their hand and buttons to press while listening. We live in a world where interpersonal communication is a dying art, and if we can get our students to focus and learn the keys, then they will have an advantage.

Once the students are focused, I ask them a question. As they answer, I nod my head and react appropriately with each of their comments. When it fits, I add short comments like, "That is so interesting," or, "Wow." These are meant to be "fillers" and are added as the person is in mid-conversation. Afterward, I answer the question, and I have a student hold a mirror behind me so the child I am talking to can see their reactions.

Each year at RCA, we have a competition that tests our students' soft skills: how to give a firm handshake, carry on a conversation, present their thoughts and ideas, use proper etiquette, etc. The event is called "The Amazing Shake," and it is set up like an obstacle course. The students have to visit fifty stations where real CEOs and business leaders are waiting to test their skills. There are numerous rounds until a winner is crowned. One year the final five were interviewed one at a time by one of Delta's vice presidents. When he announced the winner he stated that all five had been extremely charismatic and engaging...when they were talking. He said that only one of the five had been a charismatic and engaging listener, and that was the one he selected.

# RULE 38

*On a field trip, enter a public building quietly. We will enter the building so quietly that no one will even notice we are there. This rule applies to entering any place where people are gathered, whether it be the movies, a church, a theater or any other venue.*

I am sure that most teachers try to get their classes to be quiet when entering buildings and other areas while on field trips, but it is a lot easier to tell them what you expect from them before you are on the trip than to wait until you have arrived at your destination. My students also know that before we get on a subway, enter a restaurant or go into any establishment, we are going to creep in there like mice. Over the years, we have certainly gotten some shocked, impressed, and appreciative looks. Most people, when they see a huge group of kids entering their building, think, *Run for cover!* But we often take people by surprise by getting all the way into a building before they even realize we are there.

When I worked in Harlem, the local schools were invited to see a play near Times Square. When we arrived at the theater, there were about twenty other classes lined up outside waiting to get in. The students from the other schools were not behaving and there was pandemonium. I told my students to stay in a line and maintain order. I told them we would not carry ourselves like those other classes. Soon we started to file into the theater, and it was very disorganized. There was a lady trying to organize the groups and get them to their seats, but students were everywhere and no one really knew where to go. My class, observing our rule, walked in without a sound in two single-file lines. We stood near the door behind everyone else, and we waited. All of a sudden, the lady who was in charge noticed us, and she walked in our direction. She asked where the teacher was for our group; I raised my hand. She said, "Very, very nice to meet you. Come this way." We were led into the theater first and were given front-row seats.

Sometimes respect for others may not seem like it is going to have an impact, especially when you see no one around who is taking manners into consideration. However, that is usually the time when such kind actions will be most appreciated and recognized by others.

## RULE 39

*Be a good guest. When entering someone's home, abide by the Southern Three.*

I was raised that when you enter someone's home for the first time, you must abide by the Southern Three—three hospitable things you must do. The first is to take off your shoes, the second is to bring a gift (like a bottle of wine or baked goods), and the third is to compliment something. But as I have traveled with students where we have stayed in the homes of relatives or donors, I have been shocked by how little they seem to know. I even had a donor ask one of our boys, "Did you sleep well last night?" and he responded, "No, this house is scary." Oh me.

On field trips, I tell the students it is a good idea to compliment something about the place we are visiting. For example, if we visit someone's home, it is a nice gesture to tell them you think they have nice curtains. People are always self-conscious when they have guests visit their home, so you want to make them feel at ease. Also, if we are visiting other places such as a museum or theater, it is nice to comment on how beautiful the architecture is or to tell the guide that you think the facility is very nice. When we go on field trips like that, I always make sure that the students are prepared, know what they are going to see, and are given examples of things to compliment. Some may say I am putting words in their mouths, but actually, they are kids, I am their teacher, and they need practice. It is all about giving them tools they will be able to use after they leave my classroom and are no longer under my guidance.

When I visit the homes of my students' parents, I always try to put them at ease and make them feel as comfortable as possible. It is usually obvious they have spent time cleaning and preparing for the visit, and I want them to know I appreciate their efforts and that I like their home. When I walk in, I find something I like or find interesting and I let the family know it. It helps to make them feel more comfortable and relaxed.

On overnight trips, the rules are more in-depth. Prior to staying in any home we review these rules:

1. Upon entering, thank the owner of the home for allowing you to stay the night. Let them know you really appreciate the opportunity.

2. When they show you where you will sleep, act excited and say, "Oh, this will be great. Thank you so much!"

3. When you change clothes, never put pieces of clothing on the floor. Dirty clothes should always go back into your bag. (Pack an empty trash bag and place dirty items inside it.)

4. After taking a shower, never place a wet towel on the bed or on the floor. Ask the host where you should place used towels.

5. When dinner is being prepared, ask the host if you can help set the table, chop celery or whatever else seems to be needed.

6. After eating, offer to wash the dishes. The host will say you don't have to, but offer one more time. If they say no twice, then you are off the hook.

7. Keep your eye on the trash can, and, if it is full, ask the host if it's okay if you replace it and take the old trash bag out.

8. Never run or make loud noises in anyone's home. Treat it like a library.

9. If there are games to be played, ask the host if they will be on your team, and seem excited about it.

10. If you notice trash or napkins that have been left by others, pick them up and throw them away.

11. When you go to bed, go to sleep. This is not the time for laughing and giggling throughout the night, because it could disturb the sleep of the host.

12. When you wake, neatly remake the bed or roll up the sleeping bag. Place items to the side and out of the way.

13. Ask the host if they had a good night's sleep and let them know that you slept like a baby, even if that is not true.

14. When it is time to leave, thank the host for their hospitality, the wonderful food, and for opening their home to you.

15. As we pull away, if the host is waving goodbye, you should continue to wave goodbye until you can no longer see the host.

## RULE 40

*During an assembly, do not speak and do not look around and try to get the attention of your friends in other classes.*

As a student, I remember loving assemblies. As a teacher, I hate them. They disrupt the day, get the students off track, and provide many opportunities for misbehavior. Actually, those are the same reasons why I loved assemblies as a student.

To make the process more bearable, I explain to the students, in detail, exactly how I expect them to act when we are in the auditorium. On the first day of school when we come to this rule, I have the students line up and we walk to the auditorium. I have them file into our designated rows, and I have them sit facing forward with their hands in their laps. No one is to put their arms on the armrests. I then go and sit at different places in the auditorium, calling individual names, throwing paper, and doing whatever I can to get their attention. My students practice staying focused, facing forward, and not talking.

On days when we have assemblies, I remind them of our practice session, and the kids remember exactly what I expect from them. They are always on their best behavior, even in the midst of the often-chaotic auditorium.

## RULE 41

*Use appropriate phone etiquette at all times.*

Kids, unless taught otherwise, have the worst phone manners imaginable. I can't tell you how many times I have answered my phone and heard, "Mr. Clark, I don't know how to do this homework." To guide the students, I practice a simple role-play situation with them:

Phone rings.

**Mr. Clark:** "Hello, this is Mr. Clark."
**Student:** "Good evening, Mr. Clark, this is Jasmine. Is now a good time to talk?"
**Mr. Clark:** "Sure, what can I do for you?"

**Student:** "I'm having some trouble with problem #3. Could you possibly give me some direction?"

**Mr. Clark:** "Sure, what seems to be the problem?"

**Student:** "When I find the area of the triangle it seems to be too large."

**Mr. Clark:** "Oh, I bet you are forgetting to divide by 2 after you multiply the base and height."

**Student:** "Oh me, you are right. Thank you so much for helping me, Mr. Clark, and I hope you have a wonderful night. I'll see you tomorrow!"

**Mr. Clark:** "Good night, Jasmine."

**Student:** "Good night!"

I ask the students to try to make sure each of the 5 elements is included in their call:

1. An appropriate greeting
2. Identification of yourself
3. Check that it's a good time to talk
4. Present the reason for the call
5. A polite and appreciative goodbye

In the case that the person says they are busy and can't speak the student should respond by saying, "I am so sorry to have disturbed you, and my question can wait until I see you in class tomorrow. Have a good night."

It may seem elementary to have the students rehearse the script, but when I have had to tell them I was in the middle of dinner or too busy to talk, most students used to just sit silently for a moment, and then they would hang up. We should never assume students know how to handle situations. I hope the skill of proper manners on the phone will stick with them and they will use it many more times throughout their lives.

## RULE 42

*When we return from a trip, shake my hand as well as the hands of every chaperone. Thank us for taking the time to take you on the trip, and let us know you appreciate having the opportunity to go. I am not concerned with being thanked; I am concerned with teaching you that it is appropriate to show appreciation when someone has gone out of their way to help you.*

When I was growing up, my parents would always remind me to thank my teachers, Scout leaders or other adults for anything they had done to help me. If I stayed over at a friend's house, I had to thank the parents for allowing me to stay and for cooking dinner or any other thing they did for me. I was always told to thank teachers after field trips or after any special effort they made to help me. This soon became second nature.

It amazed me when I started teaching that most of my students had not been taught those same types of manners. Sometimes it was awkward to ask the students to thank me for things I was doing for them, but I had to in order to get them in the hang of doing it. Even after much practice, there were still students who would forget to thank the chaperones. It takes a lot of reinforcement before kids get the hang of it. There was one student in Harlem named Tyrone who was an exception. He wasn't one of the best students in the class in terms of behavior or academics, but every time I took students on trips, I made sure he was included. I did so because after each trip, he was always genuinely grateful to have been invited, and he would make sure to shake my hand, look me right in the eye, and tell me that he had had a great time and appreciated my time and effort. He never forgot to thank me, and so I never forgot to include him.

At RCA, we have taught our students that there are many ways to show appreciation and that you don't have to wait until the end of the trip to say thank you. I recall taking an eighth grade class to the movies, and Alec turned to me before the movie began and said, "Mr. Clark, I am so excited! Thank you so much for bringing me to see this movie." That statement meant more to me because it was genuine and in the moment than the twenty-nine handshakes I received when we returned to the school.

Other ways to show appreciation are to pay attention to tour guides, ask questions, volunteer to help pass out straws and napkins when we eat, look out the window to see the sites instead of having your head in a phone, avoid complaining, and take advantage of opportunities!

# RULE 43

*When we are on field trips and we have to go up escalators, we will stand to the right. That gives other individuals who are in a hurry the option of walking up the left-hand side of the escalator. When we are entering an elevator, the subway or a doorway, we wait for others to exit before we enter.*

After college when I moved to London, I was shocked at how polite everyone was in the subways. I was even more impressed when I traveled to Japan. In both places, people made an extra effort to make way for others and respect others' space. On escalators, everyone stood to the right and walked to the left. On elevators, everyone stood over to the side and allowed individuals to exit before they began to enter. In Japan, before the doors opened to the subways, everyone got in a single-file line and entered the train without any shoving or pushing. Can you imagine trying to explain to subway riders at Grand Central Terminal that they are going to have to get in a line and enter the subway one by one?

As I have traveled around the United States, I have been frustrated at times with the lack of respect in public places. One thing that gets to me more than other things is that most people don't seem to know that on the escalators they need to "stand right, walk left." I am usually late to catch a plane or get to a meeting, and whenever I walk up the escalator, there will be just as many people standing to the left as there are to the right. Sometimes I just want to yell out, "Stand to the right, walk to the left!" I do suppress that urge, thank goodness. I make sure to explain to my students how the system works in hopes they will help enforce it and understand the importance of respecting others' space.

I have found that if a child walks in a crowded space and someone blocks their way, they just stand and stare. I tell my students that "Excuse me" are magic words, and when they say them in a humble way and with a smile, they can part the Red Sea.

## RULE 44

*When in a line, walk single file, two to three feet behind the person in front of you with your arms at your sides. Face forward at all times. There is absolutely no talking.*

The first day I started teaching in North Carolina, I knew the other teachers and the principal were curious to see how disruptive the class would be under my inexperienced guidance. The principal had warned me how the class was, and I had seen them chaotically walk down the hall to the lunchroom the day before. I knew that when they walked down the hall under my supervision, I had to prove I could handle the class; I had to have them in a perfect line.

As we started to line up, the students were all over the place, talking and laughing and nowhere near organized. I had to do something, so I told them that we would not go to lunch until the line was perfectly straight and no one was talking. I soon realized we were going to be there quite a while, as none of the kids gave much weight to my threat. I told them that for every word someone spoke, we were going to wait one complete minute before leaving for lunch. A girl said, "Do what?" and I said, "That will be two extra minutes." Someone yelled, "Y'all better shut up, because I'm hungry," and I said, "Okay, seven extra minutes, and be glad I didn't count the contractions as two words." After about thirty minutes of this, Mrs. Briley, the head lunchroom lady, came down the hall looking for us. She was quite insistent on sticking to the schedule and she must have thought I had lost my mind.

We finally marched down the hall to lunch, forty-five minutes late. I walked at the front of the class, turned backward so I could watch them. Not a single child in the line made a sound, and as we passed the office, I saw the kids were looking fixedly at something behind me. I couldn't turn around, though, so I had to wait to finally see that they were looking at the principal, who was standing in the office doorway with a dumbfounded expression.

From that day on, the class lined up silently and with no drama. They knew my expectations and they knew I was going to stick to my guns if they didn't fall in line. It made my life easier and it brought needed structure to the day. I have always made sure my classes maintained order outside of the classroom. The way I have them march in lines makes them seem like little soldiers, and some may say it is militaristic to expect my students to march in such a way, but I think they like the order and structure. The kids seem to enjoy the organization of the line and they are proud of the way they look.

# RULE 45

*Take schoolwide drills and precautions seriously.*

When I was in elementary school, the Cold War was still going on and we would periodically have nuclear bomb drills. These were different from the ones where we would go in the hall and crouch in a ball and cover our heads. For these, we would get under our desks and cover our heads. I can still recall being eight years old, sitting under a desk and wondering, "If a nuclear bomb does hit us, how in the world is this desk going to protect me?"

Another thing I recall from those days is students giggling under desks and misbehaving. When we were crouched down in the hallway it was even worse, because Todd was always trying to break wind and make everyone laugh. For those reasons, I always make sure to explain clearly to children why we have drills, the purpose of the drills, and the rationale behind crouching, crossing a street, closing a door before exiting, and why we congregate at various parts of buildings that are more structurally sound. I want them to understand the gravity of the moment, and it helps cut down on behavior issues and students feeling like it is a waste of time.

In the home, it's important to have conversations with children about what to do if they smell smoke or hear an intruder. Having a safety plan for getting out of high windows and how to navigate a home that is engulfed in smoke is a necessary precaution. No one wants to talk about it, but children will make bad decisions, especially if they are frantic.

Preparing them ahead of time gives them a greater likelihood of remaining calm and making it to safety. And, in terms of intruders or kidnappers, parents should always have a "secret word" with their children. If a man stops your daughter while she is riding her bike and says, "Your mom was in a car accident and asked me to pick you up and take you to meet her at the hospital," the child should ask, "What's the safe word?" If the man doesn't know it, then she would know her mother didn't send him to pick her up.

This age of active shooters has added a new element to our preparations. During our active shooter training at RCA, we learned that the U.S. government recommends the following process: 1) Run, 2) Hide, 3) If you can't hide, fight. Adding the element of "fight" is something that surprised our staff members, so you can imagine sharing that with students comes as a surprise. This is all the more reason why it's important to discuss with the entire school. Realizing you actually might need to go on the offensive, if running or hiding isn't an option, is something people need to hear, because it isn't something that comes naturally. It saddens me greatly that these options even need to be discussed, but in today's world I feel they are necessary to note.

## RULE 46

*When we go to a movie theater, there will be no talking whatsoever. I don't care how good the movie is or what you want to say to the person beside you, you will not so much as whisper! Do not put your feet on*

*the chair in front of you. If you eat during a movie,*
*eat as quietly as possible. If you purchase candy to*
*eat during the movie, open the wrapper and have it*
*ready before the movie begins; trying to open a bag*
*of candy during a movie is very annoying to others.*
*It is also very rude to leave a cell phone on during a*
*movie.*

It always amazes me when I start to explain how I expect
my students to act when we go to the movies that they don't
understand why they can't talk when they have a question or
when they want to make a comment. They don't understand
why they can't open their candy if they are hungry or put their
feet on the chairs in front of them if they are uncomfortable.

In the popular film *Scary Movie*, there is a scene where a
girl is talking on her cell phone throughout the entire movie.
Those around her keeping telling her to hush, and she makes
the comment, "I paid my money like everybody else in here."
That scene is hilarious, but unfortunately that is the type of
attitude many real people have. I recall once attending the
movies with my friend Erica. She knows how I am about manners in the theater, and she assured me she had turned off her
cell phone. We were sitting in the crowded theater when I
heard Erica whispering. I thought she was talking to the person next to her, and I was about to nudge her to be quiet when
I noticed that she was talking on her cell phone. She looked
at me and saw that I was not happy; she whispered to me,
"What's wrong? I had it on vibrate."

It may be impossible to live in a world where theater
etiquette is observed by all, but, hopefully, pointing out to

children how they should act will make going to the movies a more positive experience for many people. The first time I took students from Harlem to the movies I spent the entire time getting them to stop talking and to pay attention. Toward the end of that school year it was a different story. We went to another movie and during the previews there was a family of three children and a mother who were sitting behind us and rambling on and on about one thing or another. I kept trying to catch the mother's eye to show her my displeasure, but she wouldn't look my way. My students sat there quietly, paying attention and trying to ignore the noise. Finally, just as the previews were ending, a group of them got my attention and said, "Mr. Clark, can we please move?" It sounded like a good idea to me, and all thirty-seven of us stood up, walked down the aisle, and moved to another area of the theater. I'm not sure if that lady took the hint, but that isn't what is important. What's important is that my kids knew the behavior of that lady and her family was wrong. Just months before that, they would have seen it as normal, and they would have acted the same way.

### RULE 47

*Do not bring Doritos into the school building.*

Even though this rule may not make sense to you, and it won't have much relevance to the general public, I couldn't write a book about my fifty-five rules without including it. I definitely get more comments and questions about this one than any other. First I will tell you how I explain this rule to my students... then I will tell you the truth about this rule.

I tell the students a true story about something that happened when I was young. My mother would buy one bag of Doritos for my sister and me to share as our after-school snack while we watched *The Flintstones*. My sister, Tassie, being greedy, would take out one chip, lick all of the cheese off it, and then place it back in the bag. She knew I would never stick my hand in the bag after that, so she would have it all to herself. As I recount the story I play up the effect it had on me; I tell my students that to this day I cannot bear to see the sight of a Doritos chip. The truth? Not really. Basically, I just wanted to have a rule that adds character and humor to the list. The little touch of personality adds something unique and quirky to the rules, and the students love it.

This rule definitely causes some commotion and gets the students talking. There are always students each year who resent not being able to bring Doritos for lunch, but I warn them repeatedly what will happen if they do. Some test me; if I see them with the chips, I walk over to them wearing an expression of disgust, snatch the bag from the table, walk over to the trash can, and bust the bag, sending chips all over the place. Sometimes in class, I notice a bag of Doritos sticking out of someone's backpack. I walk to the board and continue to teach like normal.

All of a sudden, I turn quickly to face the class and say, "No one move!" I then begin to sniff, gliding slowly to the right, slowly to the left. "Silence!" My nose will begin to lead me in the correct direction until eventually, "Aha!" I "find" the

Doritos, march over to the trash, and crush them, much to the delight of the students and, believe it or not, the enjoyment of even the student who has just lost his lunchtime snack. By the way, rumor has it in New York that Mr. Clark can smell Doritos from up to fifty feet away.

I have had teachers use my rules and procedures and later come up to me and say, "Now, Mr. Clark, I have told the kids not to bring Doritos, but I really don't understand why." I usually just laugh and then explain the story. I tell the teachers they need to develop their own Rule 47 to add their own personality. I explain that they need to make the rules their own.

I recently took a group of former students on a trip to a summer camp. I had taught these students six years prior, and had remained in contact and was still very close with them. We stopped at a convenience store and each student was allowed to get one drink and one snack. When we got to the van, I noticed that one girl had a bag of Doritos and she had a smirk on her face. I quickly took the bag from her, walked over to a trash can, and smashed the bag between my hands, to the delight of everyone in the van. I said to the girl, "Sabina, why would you get a bag of Doritos?" and she replied, "I knew you were going to do that and it was worth not getting a snack to see it again." Kids love things that are different and unusual, and by performing my "show" to enforce the Doritos rule, I add something unique and memorable to the list.

# RULE 48

*If any child in this school is bothering you, let me know. I am your teacher and I am here to look after you and protect you. I will not let anyone in this school bully you or make you feel uncomfortable. In return, I ask that you not take matters into your own hands; let me deal with the student. Do not bully others.*

This is a big rule for building morale and a family bond in the class. I want the kids to feel safe in the school, and I want them to see me as someone who will fight for them and stand up for them if the time comes. Some might say, "Mr. Clark, you should let kids fight their own battles." I feel the kids have enough battles to deal with these days, and if I step in and handle a few of them, so what? I know if I were a kid in school, it would be nice to know I had someone there to take up for me if anyone messed with me.

I remember an incident when I was in sixth grade. I stepped on Lisa's boots, and she was so angry that she said she was going to get her friends to beat me up. Well, I told my sister, Tassie, who was in high school at the time. The two schools were on the same campus, and the next day Tassie appeared at my classroom door. She told my teacher, Mrs. Woolard, that she had to give Lisa an important message from the office. Lisa walked out in the hall and to this day I have no idea what Tassie said to her. When Lisa walked back in she was white as a sheet. The message obviously wasn't from the office; it was from my big sister. She had handled the matter, and I never heard one more negative word from Lisa again.

I want to be that influence in my students' lives. I want them to know they are protected and cared for as long as they are in my class. Whenever they bring to my attention that another child in the school has bullied them in one form or another, I make sure they know that I will not stand for it and I am making it a top priority. As soon as possible, I get the two students together, usually outside of the other student's classroom.

I remember one time in Harlem when my student Jeremy told me that a kid named Mark was calling him names. During break, I walked Jeremy down the hall and pulled Mark out of his class. I told Mark what I had heard, and then I listened to his version of the story. Mark denied doing anything wrong, but nevertheless, my response was the same. I raised my eyebrow, looked as sternly as possible into Mark's eyes, and said through gritted teeth, "Well, I really don't care what happened. What I do care about is that nothing like that ever happens again. Now, I am not your teacher, but I am here to tell you right now, you see this student standing here? Well, he is my student in my classroom, and you are not going to talk to him, make fun of him or bully him, because if you do, you will have to deal with me. Is that clear?" Then I looked at Jeremy, and in the same tone I gave him the exact same talk about leaving Mark alone. I told him that if he ever did anything to Mark, he would have to deal with me as well. By speaking to both students, it balances out and seems like I am punishing the boys equally. I wouldn't want it to appear as if I were just taking up for my student and that Jeremy couldn't take care of himself. That could be embarrassing for him and make matters worse.

Children can be cruel. Shoot, adults can be too. It baffles me how people seek to uplift themselves at the detriment of others. Kids often seek to make a joke about someone else before anyone has the opportunity to make a joke about them. And groups of friends seek to find commonality in despising others.

I have a couch in the back of my room at RCA, and the instant I notice that students are saying negative things about each other, I pull the entire class to the couch. I then ask the students to tell me about kids in the class who are being supportive, kind, and helpful. The kids point out various students and say wonderful things about them. I then ask, "Is there anyone who may have some things they could work on?" Surprisingly, the students are very forthcoming. When it is revealed that some students are being unfriendly or rude, I ask the students to explain to that child why it's a problem and why they want the behavior to stop. In the safety of a group activity, the kids feel comfortable speaking out.

During the meetings, I always point out to my students that they should never pick on someone based on their appearance, family income or abilities. When students pick on others for things they can't change, I let them know that I find that simply cruel. Jokes at the expense of others are the weakest forms of humor. It's empty-minded and a cheap laugh. I make sure my students understand this, and I point out clearly that if they are laughing with those who make the jokes, then they are feeding the problem. And I tell them, "If bullies receive laughter, they seek to get more of it, and no one is safe, including you. If you laugh, you're likely to be the next brunt of the joke."

I encourage parents and teachers to be open with students about times when they themselves were bullied. I'll never forget a story my mother told me. When she was in high school her home didn't have an indoor bathroom, which at the time was a sign of elevated status. My mom's family had to use an outhouse that was far behind their home. One of the wealthy girls at her school, Darlene, once stayed overnight with my mom and knew she didn't have an indoor bathroom. One night, she and a carload of girls stopped at my mom's home and banged on the door frantically. When my mother answered the door, Darlene said, "Jean, we are in a pickle. Several of us need to use the restroom." And then with a smirk, she said, "Can we use yours?" My mom said she wanted to disappear into thin air. Darlene knew good and well she didn't have a bathroom, and yet there she was, standing before her with the sole intention of embarrassing her.

My mom's whole body was tense as she said, "Well, my dad is in there and he's going to be in there a long time so you all should go somewhere else." Darlene looked disappointed as she turned and led the girls back to her car. Mom said she could hear them all giggling as the doors closed and the car pulled away. She ran to her room and cried herself to sleep.

After I tell that story, I ask my students, "Do you want to be that type of person? Do you want to make people feel like my mom felt?" I then explain that everyone is someone's child, and potentially someone's mother or father. Everyone has people who care about them and love them. By picking on others you are not only hurting that person but you are hurting their family, and like my disdain for Darlene, those negative feelings could last for years. I then ask, "Do any of you want to have people talking about you and telling people how much you hurt them and how much they don't like you for the next fifty years?" It makes an impact.

## RULE 49

*Stand up for what you believe in. Don't take no for an answer if your heart and mind are leading you in a direction that you feel strongly about.*

I cannot tell you the number of times in my life I have wanted to do something, but everyone around me was skeptical and told me I shouldn't. I guess one of the main times was when I wanted to move to New York City and teach in Harlem; my parents and friends all told me that it was too risky and that I was crazy. I had a strong feeling, though, that it was what I was supposed to do, so I went with it, and it ended up being the best decision I could have ever made.

I want my students to have that same type of determination and conviction. If they want to do something or if they feel strongly about a cause, I want them to have the courage to stand up for their beliefs with confidence and fight for what they want.

As a teacher, I constantly have to stand up for my ideas and face conflict after conflict when others don't have the same vision. When my students went with me to Disney's

American Teacher Awards, I wanted the boys to have tuxedos so they wouldn't feel uncomfortable in a situation where every other male was wearing one. I arranged funding through a business to purchase the tuxedos, but the administration at the school thought it was a waste of money and the principal was adamant that the money would not be used in that way. She expected me to return the money to the company who had agreed to purchase the suits for the boys, and she said she was not going to change her mind. I stood my ground, however, and, with the help of others, we were able to convince the principal that the boys should have the suits. On the night of the ceremony, I knew the struggle had been worth it when I saw the looks on those boys' faces. They were all so excited and proud to be in the fancy clothes. It was a special moment for them, but if they had been wearing only a shirt and slacks as the principal had requested, they would have felt out of place and inferior. I never want my students to feel they are substandard to anyone or in any situation.

As a teacher, there are times when you not only have to fight for what you believe in but also have to stand up for your word. When I began teaching my first class, only a few students consistently brought in their homework each day and I knew I had to come up with some tactic to teach them to be more responsible. I gave them all a tiny piece of blue paper the size of a Tic Tac and told them that anyone who didn't bring it back the next day would get one hour of after-school detention. I know it seems weird, but that is exactly why I did it. I had to find some way to get their attention and to get them in the routine of having an after-school assignment, and if it meant demanding the return of a little piece of blue paper, then so be it. Basically, it was an assignment about responsibility. Of course, the students didn't understand the logic behind it, but I put the fear of a detention in them, and they knew I was serious. In addition, I talked to them about how our class was a team, and told them this was an assignment that we all could accomplish together. I said to the kids, "You don't want to be the one student who forgets the piece of paper and keeps us from having a perfect day of homework."

The next day every single student brought back their tiny pieces of paper. That is, everyone except for one student. That one student, Nancy, just happened to be the brightest, most well-behaved girl in the class. She was a quiet, sweet girl who always had her homework, and I was hesitant to give her a detention; however, the entire class watched me to see how I was going to handle the situation. If I didn't give Nancy a detention, the students would lose respect for my word. I couldn't go back on what I had said, so I sent the young girl, whose eyes were filled with tears, home with a detention letter.

The next morning when I walked in the school, I was met by my Aunt Carolyn, who was the school's secretary. She looked at me with a frantic expression and said in her southern drawl, "Ron, just go home. Let's call this one a sick day." I asked her what she was talking about, and she informed me that Nancy's mother was in the office and that she was angry. Even though I wanted to go home as my aunt recommended, I knew I had to face the music and report to the principal's office. I kept telling myself over and over as I walked down the hall, "Ron, what were you thinking? A blue piece of paper as homework was ridiculous!" As I walked in the office, the mother, Mrs. Woodson, shot me a look of hatred, and I was scared to death. We were both called in to sit with the principal, Mrs. Roberson, and she gave each of us the opportunity to voice our concerns. Mrs. Woodson went first. She said that Nancy had cried all night long because of the detention. She said she was a model student, had always completed all of her assignments, and she had never been in any disciplinary trouble. She felt that punishing her for losing a tiny piece of blue paper was ludicrous. It was obvious this woman was angry, and I was sitting there terrified of what was going to happen. I could feel tears welling up in my eyes. There were several times when Mrs. Roberson could have called on me to speak and I would have just started blubbering like a baby. Luckily, that didn't happen.

After much deliberation, Mrs. Roberson suggested that Nancy be given an extra writing assignment instead of attending detention, but I couldn't let that happen. I knew every child in that class was waiting to see if Nancy was actually going to have to go to detention, and I couldn't back down on my word. I needed those kids to know that I meant what I said. I turned in my seat, dipped my head, and said, "But Mrs. Roberson, it was an assignment on responsibility." She pondered, and then another suggestion was made to give Nancy silent lunch for a day instead of detention. Again, I stood my ground. I said, "I am so sorry to cause this trouble, but I'm trying to teach the students a life lesson about the importance of meeting expectations." Mrs. Roberson sat there, thought for a minute, and then she said to Nancy's mother, "We all love Nancy and know she is an incredible student who is always responsible. This is in no way a reflection on you or her, but Mr. Clark is trying to help all the students become as responsible as Nancy typically demonstrates, and for that reason I am going to let the detention stand." Needless to say, Mrs. Woodson was not happy, and she probably still hasn't forgotten it, but it was absolutely necessary in more ways than I could ever explain.

Nancy served her detention, and that class went on to have twenty-three days in a row where each child in the class turned in every piece of homework. I turned it into a challenge to see how many days we could all bring in all of our assignments, and it worked. I told them I believed they could do it; I cheered them on, and I jumped on the desks and sang and danced when they had all of their work. Part of the reason that they brought in all of their work was because of the fear of getting a detention; but other teachers used the same policy with far less success. The key to my getting those kids to become responsible and bring in their work was that I supported them, and I believed in them. It wouldn't have been possible, however, if I hadn't kept my word about the consequences.

Sometimes it is hard to stand up for what you believe in, and being the only one with a certain vision can be very lonely. I can only hope that I instill in my students a confidence in who they are and the things they stand for so they will have the courage to fight for their beliefs, their ideas, and their dreams.

## RULE 50

*Be positive and enjoy life. Some things just aren't worth getting upset over. Keep everything in perspective and focus on the good in your life.*

I love my parents. They are such wonderful and wise people. Whenever I have a problem or if something goes wrong, they have a magical way of showing me that it's never as bad as it seems. They have always said, "Well, Ron, these things happen. There's no need to get upset about it; we'll work through it." I cannot tell you how comforting it is to hear that.

One time when my mother was taking my sister and me to school, all of a sudden smoke started billowing out of each side of the car hood. Mom pulled over and got out to see what was going on. This was back in the good ol' days before cell phones, so Mom had to walk up the street to a local bar to use the phone. It was a very stressful situation, but my mom stayed calm and positive throughout. Dad came to pick us up, and instead of cursing or being upset that he had to leave work to come get us or that the car was in need of repair, he just asked if we were all okay, smiled, took us to school, then went back to figure out how to get the car to a service station. They have always had that type of attitude, no matter what problems we faced, large or small, and they have never gotten negative or disgruntled over issues that are out of their control.

One of the main reasons I love them so much is because of the way they view the world—with tolerance, understanding, and acceptance of all the world has to offer, good and bad. They are such positive people, even in the midst of adversity, and I have tried so hard to adopt that quality myself, and to pass it along to my students.

I once heard that a former colleague of mine was upset with me because of a comment I made that she had taken the wrong way. I am the type of person who likes everyone to be happy, and I hate the thought of having anyone angry with me. I didn't really want to apologize, because I didn't mean for what I said to be taken the way she perceived it. It was bothering me, though, and when I asked my mother for advice, she told me that I should either write an email or call the person and explain the situation and offer an apology for the misunderstanding. I decided to do both. First I wrote an email, and later I called. Neither worked to smooth over the situation, as the colleague remained cold and distant. It continued to bother me, and I again asked my mother for advice; she told me something very wise. She said, "Ron, you have taken the pressure off of your shoulders. You did the right thing; you called and made your peace. Now the burden is not on you anymore, it is on her. If she chooses to live with it, then let her, but I want you to stop worrying about it."

My mother was right. We can't let things bother us to the point that they make us sick. We have to realize there are some things we can't change, and there are times when there are no easy solutions. It is best to deal with those situations the best we can, take the pressure off of ourselves, and move on.

## RULE 51

*Live so you will never have regrets. If there is something you want to do, do it! Never let fear, doubt or other obstacles stand in your way. If there is something you want, fight for it with all of your heart. If there is something you want to do, go for it and don't stop until you make it happen. If there is something you want to be, do whatever is necessary to live out that dream.*

My greatest fear is that I am going to have regrets about the way I have led my life. When I was twenty-one years old, I found out I had a grandfather I had never met. (It's one of those family stories that's full of drama. I'll spare you.) In short, he was my biological grandfather and I desperately wanted to meet him, but I could not get up the courage to do so. I learned that he worked at a used car lot, and so I got a job at Mel's Diner, which was right across the street. I hoped for months he would come into the restaurant, but he never did. Then, I tried to get up the courage to walk over and introduce myself; after months and months of chickening out, I finally went to see him. That was on a Monday, and I learned he had died of a heart attack the previous Sunday. I was absolutely devastated. All of the times I was too scared to go meet him came flooding back to me, and I was very hard on myself for not having had the guts to talk to him. At that moment, I realized that even though I never met the man, he taught me one of the greatest lessons of my life: to live without regretting my choices or decisions. That is one of the main reasons I have lived my life the way I have. Before my grandfather's death I had always wanted to travel, but I was terrified to get on a plane. After his death I traveled extensively, lived in London, backpacked across Europe, spent time in Japan. I am so thankful I did. I know if I looked back on my life and hadn't had my adventures and travels, I would have felt my life was only half-lived.

I tell my students that story, as well as others like it, because I want them to truly understand they have to make the most of their lives and not let anything stand in the way of their dreams.

## RULE 52

*Accept that you are going to make mistakes. Learn from them and move on.*

We are only human, and parents, teachers, and students alike do things they will regret. I made mistakes my first year of teaching, I made mistakes my twenty-fourth year of teaching, and I'm sure I'll make mistakes my fortieth year of teaching, God willing. When it happens, you can't beat yourself up over it. You have to pick yourself up, learn from the experience, and move on.

The class of students I took over in my first year of teaching was a very hard group to discipline. There were thirty-four kids and at least twenty-five were hard to control. Nine had spent time in the alternative school program. To get them to focus and pay attention during lessons, I arranged the room so Steve couldn't see Bill and Aaron couldn't see Lakisha, and so on. I even had a partition in the corner where I would make an extremely rowdy student go and stand. One day around 1:30 P.M., I made a student named Jermaine stand behind that partition. I went on teaching and got really into it, and before I knew it the bell rang and it was time for the students to go home. They were dismissed and I sat at my desk, completely exhausted. I started grading papers, and around 3:15 P.M. I heard a BOOM!! I jumped out of my seat and looked in the corner to see Jermaine lying on the floor. He had fallen asleep against the wall and had slipped and knocked down the whole partition. I don't know who was scared more! I got him up and drove him home, and I swore I would never put anyone behind that partition again.

Another mistake I made that year involved another teacher at the school. Her name was Mrs. Bitterson and her classroom was right across the hall from mine. She was a much older teacher, approaching retirement, and there was no doubt she didn't approve of my teaching methods. She was especially angry with me because she was the fourth grade teacher, and she thought I was making fifth grade look too much like fun. She claimed that her students couldn't concentrate because they were too concerned with what was going on in my class across the way. We had several meetings with the principal about this, but none of the meetings turned out as Mrs. Bitterson had hoped. The principal supported me and my techniques, and Mrs. Bitterson would always make some snide remark like, "Well, I knew you were going to take up for him;

he's your golden boy!" She left each meeting with more and more resentment toward me.

One afternoon Mrs. Bitterson walked by my door with her class and threw a tennis ball into the room. I had started a tennis team with my students and apparently I had left one of the balls on the playground. She stuck her head in my room and stated, "Mr. Clark, YOU left this on the playground and one of my students could have tripped on it and been injured, and YOU could have been taken to court. How would you like THAT?" I replied, "Well, you just threw that same ball in my classroom, and you could have hit one of my students in the eye, and YOU could have been the one in court. How would YOU like THAT?" I realize now that this was a horrible response, and I should have handled the situation much differently. I was about to head into a horrid spiral of events with Mrs. Bitterson, and I didn't have the experience to know how to get myself out of it.

Later that afternoon, there was a knock at my door. I answered it, but the only thing I saw was a green package sitting on the floor. I picked it up and carried it into the room. I said with a big grin, "Look, kids, someone's given us a present." As I opened it, moths and crickets sprang out, and worms, slugs, and other bugs fell to the floor. The package was on Tamyius's desk and that poor kid just about had a heart attack, and I was not far from it. It contained no name, but it was obvious to me it was from Mrs. Bitterson, who loved science and had all types of insects and animals in her room. My kids definitely took it as a "slam" on them as well. They were anxious to get revenge, but I told them, "Students, life isn't about revenge. It's about rising above and you should never let anyone pull you down to their level." While I believed those words, I soon learned that putting them into practice could be very hard to do.

The next day, while Mrs. Bitterson's class was in the lunchroom, my students and I got an onion that we had used earlier in an experiment. We had cut the onion in half to count the rings and try to determine its age. Then with a sly grin I said, "All right... I've got an idea." With caution and cunning to rival that of James Bond (I really hammed it up for the kids' amusement), I crawled across the hallway and snuck into Mrs. Bitterson's room and wedged the pieces into the back of her top drawer. I then ran over to my students and said, "Kids, promise me you will never tell anyone what WE just did."

About two weeks passed, and I had completely forgotten about the onion. Then, one day, I noticed Mrs. Bitterson spraying her strawberry mist air freshener around her desk. (Lord knows she loved that strawberry mist.) I walked into her room and asked her what she was doing. She replied in her usual scratchy tone, "Something in here stinks, and I can't find it." Mrs. Bitterson loved a cotton plant that was hanging above her desk, and so out of pure cruelty I said, "Hmm, I think it's your cotton plant." She darted back at me, "You don't know what you're talking about, Golden Boy; cotton plants don't stink!" Later that afternoon, I saw her carrying the plant to the dumpster. Apparently, she believed I was right about where the smell was coming from, and I was really enjoying this joke, until days later when I left the school to head home. When I walked out to my car, it had been smeared from bumper to bumper with pieces of onion. Bless her heart, she had finally found that onion; she had even put pieces inside my car and in the air vents.

Well, I was not going to let her get the last word, so I scraped up the pieces of onion and took them home. I then puréed the pieces and put the mush in a container. The next morning, I made sure I was the first to arrive at school. I snuck into Mrs. Bitterson's classroom again, went to her overhead cart, and got her strawberry mist bottle. I then took the onion liquid, poured it into the bottle, and sprayed it all over her room.

When she walked into her class, she stopped abruptly; she knew I had put the onion somewhere, but for the life of her she couldn't find exactly where the smell was coming from. I had to suppress my laughter all morning as she had her kids turning the room upside down in an attempt to find the onion. All the while, she stormed from one end of the room to the other, spraying that "strawberry mist" with all her might.

It wasn't until after that event that another teacher at the school, Mrs. Zurface, sat me down and told me some things about Mrs. Bitterson that I hadn't known. She was really a very kind and generous woman, but because of certain things that had happened in her life, she didn't quite have the zest and energy she once had for education. Mrs. Zurface said that one of the reasons Mrs. Bitterson did not like me was because she wanted to teach just like me, but she didn't know how. Also, Mrs. Bitterson wanted the kids to like her, just as we all do, but she didn't know how to make that happen. Mrs. Zurface really opened my eyes, and I soon realized that I had to turn my experience with Mrs. Bitterson into a positive one. I think the best compliment we can give each other as colleagues is to ask for help, so I swallowed my pride and wandered into her room one day after school. I asked, "Mrs. Bitterson, I am trying to prepare this science lesson and it's really tricky. Could you give me some advice?" She responded, "What? The Golden Boy needs my help?" This woman was a piece of work.

She eventually helped me, and soon her frigid exterior thawed. In a short while, she was even speaking to me and laughing at my jokes. The weight of the world was off my shoulders, but the true effect was seen in the students. When Mrs. Bitterson and I got along, the kids seemed to relax. They could tell the negativity was gone, and it was as if the weight of the world was off them as well. If you don't like someone, I promise your students can sense it, and we never want children to suffer because of negative energy we create or put in their learning environment.

I could have made Mrs. Bitterson feel like she was needed. I could have respected her. Instead, I made a bad situation worse, but I learned from my mistakes.

At times, there are going to be conflicts between teachers or any two people working together. Sometimes, it is best to swallow a little pride and smooth the situation over. Asking a coworker for help or advice is a huge compliment, and it can go a long way in repairing tense relationships. Since the situation with Mrs. Bitterson, I appreciate that all teachers have advice, skills, and talents that make all of us better teachers. We just have to learn to let each other know we appreciate what we can learn from each other and there is mutual respect.

An additional detriment of not getting along with co-teachers is the impact it has on the students. One day after the onion fiasco, I saw Mrs. Bitterson telling one of my students to stop running down the hall. He looked at her like she was crazy and he kept right on going. I, of course, caught up with him and gave him a lecture he wouldn't soon forget. But the point is he had no respect for Mrs. Bitterson, and that came as a result of my treatment and opinion of her. When there is tension between teachers, the students feel it, and it makes them uncomfortable. Kids these days are witness to enough hostility; they shouldn't have to endure it at school as well. On the flip side, when teachers get along and like each other, the students feel more at peace and perform better in that type of environment. My co-teacher, Barbara Jones, and I got along so well. We were always laughing, giving high fives, and supporting each other. The students loved to be around us and they thrived when with us. That is the type of environment we should make for our kids.

Making mistakes such as leaving kids in corners or being childish with vegetables is part of life, and no matter how old or experienced we are, they will still happen. One thing for sure, though, is that with experience, there are far fewer mistakes. The longer I teach, the fewer errors I make; as the years pass, when I do make a slipup, I am much more equipped to handle it.

## RULE 53

*No matter the circumstances, always be honest. Even if you have done something wrong, it is best to admit it to me, because I will respect that, and oftentimes I will forgo any disciplinary measures because of your honesty.*

When I was teaching in New York City, my student Tamara's desk was always a source of conversation, and I have a whole list of stories about it. One day the science teacher, Mrs. Scofland, did a lesson that required the use of food coloring. When she was finished with the lesson, a small container of green food coloring was missing. I asked if anyone had it, but no one raised a hand. Later, I looked back to see that Tamara's face was completely green! She had hidden the bottle in her desk, and apparently she had spilled it all over her hands. She wasn't aware of it, but she had rested her face in her hands and her face was completely covered! I decided to ask again. "Class, are you sure that none of you have the missing container of green food coloring?" No hands rose, so I went back to teaching. A few minutes later, I couldn't stand it any longer, and I said, "Tamara, are you sure that you don't know where the food coloring is?" and she replied, "No sir," as if I were crazy to think she had it. I simply replied, "Well, Tamara, just in case you do have it in your desk, I somehow feel that you have already been punished enough." She eventually discovered it was all over her face and that I knew she had taken the container, but by then, half the school had seen her green face at lunch time.

Honesty. It's the easiest route to take. It requires no excessive thought, no elaborate plan, and no need to recall fake information. But people struggle with it, especially children.

One day a parent came to my classroom door and asked to speak to me in the hall. As I stepped outside, I told the class to get ready for lunch and not to say a word. I talked to the parent for a couple of minutes, and then I went back in the class and told the students to line up. As the kids passed me in the line, many of them were whispering out of the side of their mouths, "Candy and Grier were talking." I didn't say anything to the culprits at that time, but as Candy and Grier walked out of the room I asked them to stand over to the side so I could talk to them. I leaned down and looked them in the eyes as I said, "Girls, I know I can count on you two. Can you please tell me if anyone in the room was talking while I was in the hall?" Candy shook her head so hair bobbed from side to side as she said, "Oh no, Mr. Clark, you would have been soooo proud of everyone. We just were so busy getting ready for lunch that no one had a chance to talk at all." I looked her dead in the eye and said, "Are you sure, Candy?" and she answered, "Oh, yes, Mr. Clark. I would never lie, because my mom taught me lying is wrong, and I respect you too much to lie to you, and besides, I've read the Bible." Well, I then put on my all-hell-is-about-to-break-loose face and I said, "Well, ladies, let me tell you a little something: when I was outside, I could hear both of you talking!" Grier turned white as a sheet and she said, "Oh, I am so sorry, Mr. Clark, I was talking." I said, "Well, thank you for being honest, Grier, go on to the lunchroom." Immediately, Candy sprang into action: "Oh, Mr. Clark, I am sorry, but I was talking, too. Can I go to the lunch-room now?" Well, Candy was not going to get off that easy. "Candy," I said, "you stood right here and told me you weren't talking and that you definitely wouldn't lie about it because your mother taught you not to lie and that you respect me so much and that you have read the Bible. I want to hear just what you have to say for yourself, young lady!" Candy hung her head for a couple of seconds, and then she said quietly, "Well, I didn't read the whole Bible."

Honesty. It is the key to having a successful year in my classroom. On the first day of school, I spend a lot of time explaining to the kids that sometimes it is worth getting in a little trouble by telling the truth so you can have an easy conscience. I tell them it is far more important to tell the truth, because then they will be respected and trusted, and those two qualities can go a very long way.

I always make a point to reward honesty. Sometimes students do things that make me want to discipline them, but I won't because they were honest about what they did. In my eyes, that is a far greater lesson to learn.

Kids are skeptical at first, and they lie through their teeth to avoid getting into trouble. It takes a lot of time and patience before they realize they can tell the truth and avoid stricter punishments because of their honesty.

## RULE 54

*Carpe diem. You only live today once, so don't waste it. Life is made up of special moments, many of which happen when caution is thrown to the wind and people take action and seize the day.*

This rule sounds very similar to Rule 51, but they are really two very different things in my eyes and deserve to be separate lessons. Rule 51 is about living the life you want. This rule, carpe diem, is about living each day to the fullest and appreciating each moment.

My students must hear this a thousand times a year. It is part of who I am as a teacher and a person; it is the way I live my life and it is my wish for my students that they can learn how important it is to make the most of each and every day of their lives. When I took a group of nine students from Harlem to North Carolina for a week, I just packed them in a van and we took off for a trip that I know changed their lives forever. Before we left New York, I said to the kids, "We are going to make the most of this week. We are going to live each day to the fullest, and anything you get the chance to do in North Carolina, I want you to do it; even if it is new or different or scary, I want you to go for it!" I had them make a pact with me that during the week we would all live up to the carpe diem philosophy. They didn't let me down. Kids who were afraid of heights climbed rock walls, kids who had never been in water learned to water ski, and kids who had never eaten pig at a hog cooking asked if they could eat the tongue... and they did! It was a wild week of adventure, fun, and new experiences. We finished off the week at an amusement park. Now, I do not like roller coasters; they scare me to death. I was going to break the pact because of my fear. Can you believe it? I was going to be the one to let the group down and not live up to my own advice. I couldn't help it, I was just so terrified. Then one of my students looked at me and quoted a line I had said to him many times before, "Mr. Clark, you better get busy living or get busy dying."

My own words, back in my face—and they worked. I found myself, with the kids at my side, getting on each and every ride. I had never really enjoyed amusement parks before that day, but because I abandoned all fear and got busy living, I loved every minute of it. That week, we were all living.

How wonderful it would be to live an entire life with such freedom to try new things, experience the unknown, and face our fears. It is hard for many adults to step out there and take those chances, but kids are more willing to release their inhibitions and truly live life. If we can teach them to embrace that feeling when they are young, hopefully it will stay with them for the rest of their lives.

## RULE 55

*Be the best person you can be.*

Throughout life, you are going to be lonely at times, you are going to have your heart broken on occasion, and you are going to feel as if something is missing from your life. No life is lived without some amount of pain and heartache. No matter how bad things get, however, make sure you are always developing into the kind of person you want to be, and the kind of person others want to be around. It is important not to let external factors keep you from developing who you are and the person you are trying to become. Always make sure there are seven things in your life at all times: laughter, family, adventure, good food, challenge, change, and the quest for knowledge. With those things you will grow, enjoy life, and become the type of person you can be proud of. You will also be in a better position to help others, give advice, and learn from your mistakes because you will be a stronger, healthier, and happier person.

# TWO MORE ESSENTIALS

It's been years since I first started using The Essential 55, and since then we have added many more rules to the list at RCA. In fact, we also added three additional days of school at the beginning of the year where all we do is teach the rules of our school and role-play The Essential 55. The amount of detail we have added has grown, and I want to include a couple of the "rules" that have become guiding principles and life lessons that we work hard to ingrain in our students. You've seen new rules sprinkled throughout this book, but here are two that deserve their own section.

## BONUS RULE 1

*Rise above the salt.*

There are people in our lives that I refer to as "salt." They are negative forces of energy who spread their poison and make our lives difficult. I tell my students that no matter who they are or what roads they walk in life, they will encounter these people.

I worked for five years across the hall from one of these "salt" individuals. She couldn't stand me and she didn't hold her tongue about it. She complained that I was always "doing the hoochie-coochie dance" in my classroom and that my methods weren't appropriate. She had taught for what seemed like thirty thousand years and we were simply on opposite pages. It got to the point where she made me physically ill. When I saw her, I literally could feel my energy drain away. When I found myself walking down the hallway and saw her coming, I would dart into the bathroom or whatever room was closest. I'd lie in bed at night and dream of scenarios for how she might leave the school. I envisioned her retiring or moving to live with her sister in Florida, and I convinced myself that if she would just leave, my life would be perfect.

When I look back now, I realize just how insignificant she was, and I have no idea why I allowed her to have so much power over my life. She didn't deserve it! We only live once, and none of us should ever allow someone insignificant to have that much power over our lives. Do you know how much power we should give people who try to bring us down? You should give them the power of a small grain of salt. It's infinitesimal and harmless. Such people don't deserve to have any influence over your happiness. Ignore them.

But...on the surface I do expect you to be nice to them. I may pass someone in the hall and say, "Good morning," with a big grin, but as they walk away, I think to myself, "SALT," and keep on trucking!

I talk about this with my students a lot. I express that they won't like everyone they have to interact with in life, but they should respect that individual and treat them with kindness. Above all else, I beg of my students to never let anyone steal their joy. Life is too short and we simply don't have time to give any bit of ourselves or our lives to salt.

## BONUS RULE 2

*Be pizza, NOT BREAD!*

At RCA, we encourage our students to abide by the school's motto of "No Fear," and we ask them never to hesitate to share who they are with the world. We hope to build leaders who aren't afraid to go for it and be bold with their decisions and thought processes. With that in mind, we seek every opportunity to allow our students to make choices and give feedback about things that occur at our school. I often ask them to be "pizza" and not "bread." Bread is safe, normal, and basic. People like bread, so if you present bread to them (a basic effort) then it's pretty much what they expect and they won't complain. At RCA, however, we beg our students to be pizza, to be alive, zesty, and full of flavor and surprises. The problem is that sometimes pizza gives people indigestion and can cause issues.

For students, being pizza means having the courage to offer your opinions in class discussion. Pizza students aren't afraid to take up for others who are being mistreated. When the teacher tells the class it's not necessary to add color to their drawings, the pizza student goes the extra mile and adds color. While a bread student wishes their school had a certain club, the pizza student will take steps to start the club themselves.

For teachers, many of us struggle with a generation of children who are being coddled in their homes. There are parents in America more concerned with the self-esteem of their children than if they are being challenged and given an outstanding education. This is typical behavior in a nation that is the world's superpower; when parents have more than their parents could give them, they tend to give too much to their own children. The children, in turn, become entitled and lack a work ethic. Parents become less concerned with academic success and more concerned with their child receiving the status of being on the honor roll. It's a crisis.

When teachers try to challenge students and grades fall, parents show up in the principal's office and teachers are asked, "What's wrong with your teaching methods that the students aren't having more success?" Many teachers are so bothered by this they have left the profession. Others have resigned themselves to just making the work easier so students will all receive better grades. Many have resorted to allowing students to retake tests over and over until students achieve success and get good scores. And what is the outcome? The United States has fallen to twenty-ninth in the world in terms of test scores, and we continue to drop. This concerns me so much because the strength of our country relies on the strength of our education system. It is the biggest indicator of where our country will be ten, twenty or thirty years from now. And y'all, when I am in a rest home, I personally don't want uneducated people taking care of me. Do you?

In light of this parental pressure, many teachers decide to be bread. They play it safe, use basic lessons, and don't go above and beyond. Parents don't complain because the grades are good and they don't expect more. I beg my teachers, my students, and everyone I know to be PIZZA! Be bigger, better, bolder! A pizza teacher may decide to take students on a field trip where they get hands-on learning and have a good time, but when she returns thirty minutes late with the students because of traffic, parents complain. The next day the teacher has a meeting with the principal where she is told she can't take more field trips if the students can't be brought back on time. The teacher walks out of that meeting thinking, "If I had only been bread, this wouldn't have happened."

Yes, there are risks to being pizza. You will get your feelings hurt, make mistakes, and find disappointments along the way. But my goodness it is an electric experience being PIZZA! What the education profession and our country need at this time are people who are inventive, forward-thinking, and alive with new ideas of tomorrow! We don't need status-quo bread. I am begging everyone who reads this to be pizza and to encourage the children in your life to be pizza—to be more, to be a world-changer.

When you look back on your life, I promise you, if you lived a life of bread you will regret it and wish you could go back and try it all again. If you live a life of pizza, I daresay that you will be an eighty-five-year-old with a smile on your face. And if we as a collective nation seek to live an existence of pizza, I think our country will be all the better for it.

# A FEW TIPS FOR DEALING
# WITH CHILDREN

Journal entry:

I can't sleep. Tomorrow is the first day of school, it's 3:30 A.M. and I am too nervous to get any rest. Even if I do fall asleep, I will probably have the dream again where I realize I have left my class alone somewhere in the school, and I can't find them. I just keep running up and down the halls, terrified because I have left them unsupervised. I finally find the kids, and they have been in my class the entire time. I was the one who was lost, and I was in the wrong place, not the students. As I walk in, I see that the principal has discovered the unattended class, and she is standing at the front of the room with her arms crossed and a disgruntled expression on her face.

### *NIGHTMARE!*

I know that dream is all about my fear that I am going to fail my students, that I am not going to be there for them. I am afraid the students won't like me, that they aren't going to listen to me, and that I won't be able to reach them. I am scared to death that I am going to fail...

That nightmare is one I used to have repeatedly, and that is an actual excerpt from my journal. You might think I wrote it on the night before my first day as a teacher; it was actually written just before the first day of my seventh year in the classroom. Working with kids is nerve-racking. No matter how much practice or experience you have, there are always worries and the fear you will do something wrong. That is understandable, because there is no responsibility greater than raising children. Whether you are a parent, a teacher, a counselor, or a member of the community, you face the task of setting a positive example for children, motivating them to succeed, and making a difference in their lives.

During my years of working with students and all we went through together, I learned a lot about what makes kids tick and what methods are best when it comes to handling different situations. One thing I know for certain is that when you work with kids, you have to be clever. Overall, there are four universal truths I have gathered about kids.

## 1. Kids need and like structure.

Students like to feel they are safe and that there is a figure of authority in control. I have seen teachers, as well as parents, make the mistake of being too lenient to win the affection of children. First-year teachers have said to me that they don't want to be too strict, because they want the students to like them. In the beginning, I think students do like those teachers, but in the end, they have no respect for them. The best result is to have students who like you and respect you. To do that, you have to create structure in the classroom, you have to have clear, defined rules, and you have to make the students feel safe and comfortable.

My class in Harlem was so challenging, but after I had taught and enforced the rules for a few weeks, the students were focused, respectful, and on task. One of the boys said, "Mr. Clark, I like school now because I can focus and ain't no one bothering me." I had to respond, "But you were the worst one!" A lot of teachers, especially new ones, think students want freedom, when in actuality what they really want is structure, guidelines, and, above all else, safety.

## 2. Kids will work hard for you, if they like who you are as a person.

Having a good discipline program garners respect, but you may still have kids who do not particularly like you. Getting kids to like you can be quite a task. During the summer, before I ever meet my new class of students, I send them letters so they will already know about me and my personality before the first day of school. I make sure to include lots of pictures in the letter that show I like to have fun and do exciting things. On the first day of school, I show the students pictures of me and places I have traveled. I have photos on the Promethean Board that show me when I was their age. I want the kids to immediately make a connection to me; I want them to see I am real and more than just their teacher.

Another tactic I use to get kids to like me is to do anything to get their attention, no matter how foolish it makes me look or how embarrassing it may be. I am shameless when I am with them. Sacrificing a little dignity can go a long way when trying to win over students. I can remember how my mother used to tuck me in each night when I was little. She would go to take off my socks, then act like they were impossible to get off. She would pull and pull and they would stretch and stretch. The facial expressions she would make were the funniest things I had ever seen in my life. In the end, the socks would fly off and she would tumble onto the bed. Did she look like a fool doing that? Yes. Did I love her for it? Most definitely. When I stand in front of the classroom, I let down my guard. I have no inhibitions, I put on those funny faces, I tumble to the floor, and I am willing to do whatever it takes to get through to the students.

One final thing I do to get kids to like me may seem strange, but it works. I give them a speech on the first day of school that goes something like this:

"I don't care if you don't like me. I couldn't care less. I am not here to be friends with any of you either. I have plenty of friends and I don't need any more. I don't care if you get mad and call me bad names in your mind. You are more than welcome to do that, because my objective here isn't to have you like me; it's to have you learn. I care about each and every one of you, and I am dedicated and driven to give you the best education possible. I want each of you to know I am going to do whatever it takes to make that happen, and nothing is going to stand in my way."

That may seem a bit harsh, but it is an important speech

for many reasons. First, it lets the kids know they will not get away with foolishness in the classroom, but at the same time, they know I care about them and that I am driven and dedicated to giving them the best education possible. It shows the kids where my priorities are, and it lays the groundwork for the type of year we are going to have. The funny thing about the speech, though, is that I am telling them just as hard as I can that I don't care if they don't like me, but at the same time, I am working my butt off to be the type of teacher they will like. I'm giving slide shows, dancing, standing on chairs, singing, acting, you name it.

Do I want the kids to like me? Yes, it is absolutely necessary. Do I let them know that? No. When kids know you want them to like you, you are giving them powerful ammunition to use against you, and, in the end, they could, and probably will, take advantage of that. Telling them the "story" of how you couldn't care less if they like you or not gives you the upper hand. You can't discipline kids and not love them, and you can't love them and not discipline them. The two must go hand in hand.

## 3. Kids like to know what is expected of them.

It's unrealistic to expect kids to automatically behave exactly as you hope they will. Kids are kids, and many actions that seem like common sense to us seem foreign to them. I find that no matter who the child is, if you explain exactly what you want from him and exactly how you hope he will act, he then will try his best to perform up to your standards. Often, children who are in trouble ask, "What did I do?" or say, "I didn't do anything." These kids honestly don't understand what they did wrong, and if they don't understand that their action was inappropriate, how were they supposed to know not to do it in the first place? We must be specific when we tell kids what we expect from them. We have to spell it out clearly so that there is no question in the children's minds when it comes to what is right or wrong.

During my first couple of years as a teacher, I would see a child do something wrong and I would immediately give punishments such as silent lunch or no recess. Kids like Tyquad—who when punished scrunched up his face each and every time as if he were constipated—would angrily take the disciplinary action. I learned after a while that no lesson was really being learned in these cases. Often, the kids didn't even understand why their actions made me so upset. They didn't understand what they had done wrong. I eventually talked one-on-one with kids about what had happened. One of the first things I always say is, "Tell me what you think you did wrong," or, "Tell me why you think I am upset." It is always very advantageous to hear the kid's take on the situation. Most always you will have two completely different views about what happened—theirs and yours—and if you don't take the time to explain why you are upset, then the student will continue to harbor anger or resentment toward you for the punishment. Kids definitely want to know what is expected of them; when they do something wrong, it is important to explain why their actions are inappropriate to avoid it happening again.

## 4. Kids like to know they are cared for.

In my first year of teaching, there was a child named Raymond who was a very disrespectful and disruptive child. In the classroom he was a leader to other students, and the chaos he created affected the climate of the entire class. I knew if I found a way to reach him, it would go a long way in terms of helping to control the entire class. One Friday afternoon, Raymond told me in a very cocky tone that he wasn't going to complete his weekend homework because he had basketball games to play on Saturday and Sunday in the recreation league. I didn't argue with him. Instead, I found out where the games were to be played and I attended the games. When Raymond saw me, he was shocked and asked what I was doing there. I told him I was there to cheer him on, and he couldn't believe it. Throughout the games, every time he made a shot, dribbled the ball, made a steal or got a rebound, he would glance over to see if I was watching. My being there that day meant a great deal to Raymond, and that Monday he came in with homework completed, neat and correct. He became respectful and hardworking, and he no longer was a source of negative leadership; on the contrary, he became a positive role model for the rest of the class. The previous year he had scored better than only sixteen percent of all fourth graders in the state on the end-of-year reading test. At the end of the fifth-grade year, he scored better than sixty-eight percent of all fifth graders. That improvement came simply because I showed him I cared for him, and that sparked him to perform.

It seems simple, and it is. Kids want to know you care for them. Before they will invest effort in what you say and teach, they want to know you will make an investment in them. Once you have done that, dealing with kids is a much easier, more productive, and more meaningful experience.

# TIPS FOR DEALING
# WITH PARENTS

For a classroom discipline plan to work, it is imperative to have the support of the parents. Their backing and belief in your judgment goes a long way toward an enjoyable and hassle-free year. However, if the right relationship isn't developed, dealing with parents can honestly be one of the worst parts of being a teacher. I, for one, have dozens of horror stories. Fortunately, most of them happened in my first couple of years of teaching, and I was able to learn from them and change the way I interacted with parents; however, no matter how much experience you have or how well you build a relationship with parents, in the end, problems inevitably arise.

In my first year of teaching, there was a parent, Mrs. Cleveland, who felt I was far too strict with her son. She said I gave too much homework and my academic expectations were ridiculous. She ranted and raved and met with the principal, but her efforts got her nowhere. While watching TV one afternoon, she saw a commercial that said, "If you have an emergency, call 911." Feeling her dilemma had reached emergency status, she called

911 and reported me. The police, having to follow through with the call, showed up at my classroom door. I just about fell out when they told me why they were there. Mrs. Cleveland was called to the school and she met with the principal, the police, and the guidance counselor, and they informed her why it was not appropriate to call 911 because she was unhappy with her child's teacher. She called 911 again the next week, on the cafeteria food. It somehow made me feel much, much better.

I recall a student in my class named Darnell who was a major discipline problem. I had managed to contact all my students' parents, but his phone was disconnected and I wasn't sure he was giving his mother any of the messages I sent home with him. Finally, after weeks of trying, I got his mother on the phone. The conversation went something like this:

**Mrs. Cob:** "Hello."

**Me:** "May I speak with Mrs. Cob?"

**Mrs. Cob:** "Who's this?"

**Me:** "This is Mr. Clark, Darnell's teacher."

**Mrs. Cob:** "WHO?"

**Me:** "I am Mr. Clark, Darnell's teacher."

**Mrs. Cob:** "Uh-huh, what has he done?"

**Me:** "Well, let me tell you. He has been extremely disrespectful to his classmates and me, he isn't doing his homework, and it's nearly impossible to get him to do anything I ask."

**Mrs. Cob:** "Well, you know what? He does the same types of things when he is at home with me and I have to deal with it while he's here, so you deal with him while he's there." *Click.*

That conversation may sound unbelievable, but I have encountered several parents who have that same mentality. Some see school as an extended day care service. Others view teachers as the help. It is a constant struggle for teachers to gain respect. I actually learned a lot from the conversation with Mrs. Cob, and the next year when I encountered a similar problem with a very unruly child named Trey, I handled the situation quite differently.

| | |
|---|---|
| **Mrs. Banks:** | "Hello." |
| **Me:** | "Can I speak with Mrs. Banks?" |
| **Mrs. Banks:** | "Who's this?" |
| **Me:** | "This is Mr. Clark, Trey's teacher." |
| **Mrs. Banks:** | "Uh-huh, what did he do now?" |
| **Me:** | "Actually, I was just calling to let you know how much I am enjoying having Trey in class. He gets very excited about learning and he brings a lot of energy to classroom discussions." |
| **Mrs. Banks:** | "Really?" |
| **Me:** | "Oh yes, and I told him today, I said, 'Trey, your energy and excitement about learning are refreshing,' and it was then that I decided to call you to thank you in person for the great job you have done with Trey." |
| **Mrs. Banks:** | "For real? Oh, thank you so much for sharing." |

**Me:**            "He is definitely a pleasure to teach, but I was hoping you could help me with something. Trey is having some issues getting along with his classmates. I caught him calling some students names and he isn't as polite as he should be when working in groups. He's such a great kid with a wonderful thirst for learning, and I don't want any behavior issues to get in the way of his success."

**Mrs. Banks:**    "Hold on, Mr. Clark... *Trey!! Get your butt in here right now!!!*"

When you show a parent you see good in their child, they are more willing to support you. If you never take the time to let them know you see their child's potential, they are always less likely to come to your aid.

As I said, even after years of working with parents, there are still times when conflicts arise. The second year I taught in Harlem, there was a father who scared the crap out of me. I began to think his favorite pastime was leaving threatening messages on my answering machine. If he thought I gave his daughter, Francisca, too much homework, I heard about how he could twist my body in three different directions. I am not even going to lie about it, I avoided that man at all costs, but there were, unfortunately, times when I had to meet with him.

Once I took Francisca on a field trip with five other students. I took them out to eat in a nice restaurant and to the movies, and I paid for the entire trip. All I asked of the parents was that they pick up their children at the subway stop at 8:00 P.M.

Well, at 8:30 P.M., I was still sitting there with Francisca. I got her to call her mom, and fifteen minutes later her parents showed up, and they were furious. They thought I was going to walk each child home. I explained to them how it stated on the permission slip they signed that they were to pick her up at the station. Their only defense was they hadn't read it, and they thought it was extremely rude and unprofessional that I had not taken each child home.

You may wonder why I would pick Francisca to go on a trip like that in the first place. Well, she was an absolutely wonderful student and person, and I knew she needed to have that type of experience. She was probably one of the most gifted students I have ever taught. Fortunately for her, her parents, although fond of threatening me at every turn, were willing to allow me to take Francisca on trips. They wanted the best for her, and knew the trips and activities I got her involved in were going to benefit her in many ways. They even allowed me to take her, along with a group of eight other students, on a week-long trip to North Carolina. Francisca absorbed every experience on that trip, from learning to water ski to rolling down sand dunes, from riding four-wheelers to attending a pig pickin'—a southern tradition. She really came to life that week, and I know the experience will live with her forever.

The trip was at no cost to her parents, and I expected them to at least show some appreciation when I returned Francisca home. However, her father misunderstood the time of arrival and had to wait for us at the school for hours before we arrived. He was furious with me, and proceeded to let me know, in front of the other parents, how inconvenienced he had been having to wait there for us and that I should get my act together.

He included several examples of profanity in his monologue. I apologized and kept the picture in my mind of Francisca laughing as she rolled down those sand dunes.

Why am I sharing these horrible stories? Well, to be honest, whenever I have problems with parents like the ones I mentioned, the one thing that makes me feel better is listening to other teachers share similar stories. It helps to know that others encounter the same type of parents and that it is inevitable. Hopefully, by sharing some of my trials, it helps others when they face their own difficult situations.

I have, by an overwhelming percentage, far more stories of parents who were supportive, helpful, and a pleasure to work with. I have had parents as chaperones on trips who were so wonderful and supportive of me that it was overwhelming what they were willing to put up with and the tasks they were willing to take on to help out. I have called parents at 9:00 P.M. to organize an emergency bake sale for the next day for one reason or another, and they show up at my door the next morning holding trays of cupcakes. I asked one parent to drive an hour away to pick up 500 doughnuts in her minivan. She did, but doughnut glaze seeped all over her seats. She told me it was fine, and, the next time we sold doughnuts, she was the first one to volunteer to pick them up.

The best thing parents can do for me, however, is give me their trust. No matter how much the students like you, there will be times when they feel they have been "done wrong." A lower score than they expected, a punishment they deem too harsh, or simply not calling on them enough to answer questions gives kids enough reason to despise the ground you walk on. I absolutely loved my sixth-grade teacher, Mrs. Woolard. She was one of my favorite teachers of all time; however, when I recently read back through my sixth-grade diary she had us keep, I found one passage where I wrote: "Today was horrible. I raised my hand over and over and Mrs. Woolard called on other students first. I hate that woman!" Oh, the twisted and fickle mind of a sixth grader.

The wonderful thing about kids, though, is that those feelings usually only last a few hours, and then they love you again. The problem is, before switching back to loving you again, they have usually shared with their parents how horrible a teacher you are. This is where that trust comes into play. I tell the parents at the beginning of the year to expect their kids to say I am too harsh or to complain about the amount of work I assign. I also ask them to trust I know what I am doing. The parents who understand that are a blessing, but there are some who believe whatever their child says and are quick to jump to his or her defense. Many times they call and won't even ask me for my side of the story. They assume that events happened in exactly the way their child stated. Again, these parents, for the most part, are in the minority. I have thoroughly enjoyed working with numerous parents who made my job and my life a lot easier.

There are five things I like to ask of the parents of my students:

1. If you have problems with me or how I teach, do not call the principal immediately. Call me first and give me the chance to discuss your concerns with you.

2. If you need to talk to me, email, text, or send a note with your child. I'll write back and we can arrange a time to meet. Do not show up at the classroom door unannounced for a conference. I have a classroom full of students, and when parents want "one second" of a teacher's time, it's never really one second. It's usually a few minutes, and with thirty kids waiting for me to begin a lesson, I won't be able to give the issue and the parent the time they deserve.

3. Your child should not be late or miss school for anything other than sickness or a death in the family. Allowing your child to miss school because he needs to get a haircut or go clothes shopping is sending the message that you don't value their education, and so they won't either.

4. Realize your child is one of many I teach each day; it is not always possible to address each and every need he or she may have. The sole responsibility of educating children is not the teacher's alone; it is the parents' as well.

5. Trust that I know what I am doing.

And, for the teachers who deal with extremely difficult parents, I can offer six points of advice where they are concerned:

1. Make sure your initial contact with parents is a positive one, with no negativity at all. Prior to this contact, research and find out the names of each child's parents. Don't assume that because you teach Brad Jones that his parent is Mrs. Jones. She doesn't even like that man and she sure didn't marry him. If you call her Mrs. Jones, she will respond to you, but she may not respect you very much.

2. Any time you talk with parents, the first comment about their child's performance in the classroom should be a positive one. (John may have failed every class, but if he did a good job on an art project, talk about that first.)

3. Wear professional attire. I find when I dress in a suit and tie, the students and their parents treat me with more respect. During class, I have far fewer discipline problems; when talking with parents, their overall tone is more respectful and cooperative. Teachers who want to be treated like professionals should dress and act like professionals.

4. Send notes home with students or call parents out of the blue to tell them something good their child did. I find parents always comment about how no teacher ever did that before. Parents love to hear good things about their kids and it goes a long way toward building a good relationship between you and the parents.

5. Take every possible opportunity to thank parents. If they donate supplies to the class, help with a party, chaperone a trip or make any other contribution to the class, send them a thank-you note. It makes them feel appreciated, and they are far more likely to help out in the future.

6. If a parent is extremely difficult to get along with, don't be afraid to schedule a meeting with the principal where you can express your concerns. If that doesn't work, avoid that parent like the plague. Any contact with him or her should be made through written notes. Don't put yourself through the torture.

# TIPS FOR SETTING PUNISHMENTS AND REWARDS

When developing consequences, I make them as simple and as easy for me to deliver as possible. I don't want to get bogged down with punishing students and putting stars by names or keeping up with stickers on charts on their desks. It has to be quick and easy. I decided the most efficient way if a student breaks a rule is to place his name on the board. This is only a warning. The second time I have to reprimand a student, he receives a check. For each additional infraction, additional checks are given. The consequences are as follows:

**Name on Board.**

Warning; no consequences other than the name being on the board.

At lunchtime, I make a note of the students listed and how many checks each one has. All students who have at least one check have to sit with me at lunch. I usually pick a table off to the side. No talking whatsoever is allowed. If a student laughs or says one word, he is given another day of silent lunch.

Students with two checks lose recess. If the students go to recess with another teacher, I keep the punished students in the room with me. If I go outside with the class, I instruct the students who lost their recess to sit along the side of the fence. If there is no recess because of rain, the students lose part of their gym time. Some parents may say it is cruel to take away recess from kids, but I say to them, "Listen, we are fighting in the trenches here. Teaching isn't easy, and sometimes we have to do what is necessary to get the kids to behave."

Before I started teaching the class myself, I watched Mrs. Waddle take away kids' recess periods and I thought, *That monster.* Two weeks later I found myself saying, after a student had stuck another kid with a pencil after being warned three times not to, "All right, Danyell, you just lost your recess!" It is a different world when you are the teacher and you do whatever it takes to maintain order in that classroom.

With three checks by their names, students receive after-school detention. They first are given a letter for their parents that states something like this:

> *Dear Parent/Guardian,*
> *Your child will serve detention on <u>April 5th</u> from 3:00 P.M. to 4:00 P.M. in Mr. Clark's classroom. The reason for this detention is:*
> *_____  Did not have homework*
> *Missing assignment:_____*
> *_____  Behavior*
> *Explanation: _____*
> *_____*
> *Please sign below giving your child permission to attend.*
> *Sign: _____ Date: _____*

I always make sure I have talked to the parents and explain how detention works. I never send home a detention letter unless I have spoken already with the parents and make sure they are comfortable with the punishment. Most parents are willing to allow their children to stay after school to serve the detention, but there are some who aren't. In Harlem, most students could just walk home after detention, so the parents didn't mind. In North Carolina, however, the school was in a rural area; having students stay until 4:00 P.M. meant the parents had to make a special trip to drive to the school to pick up their child. Some parents saw this as an inconvenience to them and not the student. I felt that if the child wasn't prepared for school each day, some of the responsibility should fall on the parent, and therefore I liked the punishment. If the parents, however, are absolutely adamant about the child not serving detention, then I find a punishment that is equally effective. For example, I make a deal with the parent that the student will be assigned a three-page report on a certain topic, usually one that deals with a subject we are studying in school. The child is given two days to complete the report. The deal is, if it is not completed, then the child has to serve the day of detention. About ninety percent of the time the report is not completed and the parent has to concede and allow the child to stay for detention.

If you have to substitute punishments, make sure it is something comparable in terms of the student's not wanting to do it. If students see that others do not have to deal with the consequences, then you have to make sure you can explain to them what the alternative punishment is. And listen, if other students see that some of the kids get out of serving detention and they start to argue and ask you about it, just say, "Ohhhh, is that so? You think he is getting out of detention? Well, first of all, you have no idea how bad his punishment is. Second, don't be so sure he is missing detention. And third of all, it is none of your business." The kid being punished might not serve the detention, but you can't let on that is the case. I mean, the kid might tell everyone he doesn't have to go and he gets an alternate punishment, but you just keep playing the game as if that boy just doesn't know what's in store for him.

I know it seems strange, but it works. Just never tell the class you substitute punishments for certain people.

Usually after I give out a detention slip, the student tries very hard to behave, and rarely does anyone get four checks. I tell the students that with four checks, there is an immediate parent-teacher conference about their behavior. When it happens, depending on the severity of the action, different forms of parent contact occur. If I don't feel the behavior is a serious problem, I wait and call the parent when I get home. If it is more of a problem, I call during planning time or after school. On some occasions, I ask the child to step out in the hall, and I call the parent on my cell phone. I don't do that often, because it interrupts the class. However, I do it every now and then because I want the students to know that if I need to, I can have their parents on the phone at a moment's notice. There have been times when a student's behavior warrants a parent-teacher conference with the principal present. When this happens, I make sure to have documentation of the student's behavior. For example, I have a list of each day the child had silent lunch, copies of signed detention slips, and a written explanation of the actions that led up to the four checks.

These consequences may seem harsh, and, honestly, for the first few weeks of school I always have half of the class sitting with me at silent lunch, missing recess, and spending days in detention. After about a month, though, everyone understands what they need to do to avoid getting in trouble, and there are far fewer punishments to hand out. There is a lot of work for the teacher in the beginning, but, in the end, it all pays off.

The consequences are necessary; they are the key to getting kids to perform. Each year, before going over the rules, I give a speech to the students. The message is one I deliver several times throughout the year. I believe it when I say it to the students, so I say it with passion and they know I mean it. It goes something like this:

"This year has the possibility of being one of the best years of your life. If you are willing to listen to me and do as I ask, we can make amazing things happen. You have got to believe me, and you have got to trust me. I am going to give 110 percent and work my hardest to make sure you get the best education possible. I don't care what kind of grades you have had in the past, and I don't care what kind of trouble you have been in before; this is a new year, and we are going to have a new start. And I assure you, if you are willing to follow the rules and procedures and try your best, this year you will all be stars. Not only can we be the best class in this school, we can be the best class in this country."

It may seem hokey, but I honestly believe it is possible and, therefore, it *is* possible. I believe it no matter which thirty kids in the country are in my classroom.

It is important I deliver my message in a certain way; as I say these words I am animated, moving from side to side, looking the students in the eye, and speaking with conviction. As I look around the room, I see in their faces they are starting to believe it. Why? Well, because quite simply, they want to believe it is possible; they want to believe it is true.

A final component to getting children to perform involves giving rewards. When students do well, let them know it. One of the main rewards I use is good old-fashioned praise. In all opportunities possible, I let kids know the things they have done well and the talents they have in certain areas. I find it is effective to praise a child one on one, but I have seen the biggest influence on students is when I give them accolades in front of others. Praise in front of other students is a very powerful persuasion technique.

When I taught in North Carolina, there was a child named Arlis who did poorly at most subjects. He was a solid D student and quite often he failed the majority of his courses. In North Carolina, fifth-grade students have to take end-of-year tests in math and reading. To be on grade level, you must score a level 3; to score a level 4 means you are above grade level. Levels 1 and 2 designate students who are below grade level; those in level 1 are required to attend summer school or repeat the grade. The year before, Arlis had scored low level 2s, and even though I saw a great deal of potential in him, he was very disinterested in school. I was afraid he would fall in the level 1 category in fifth grade.

In the first month of the school year, we read *The Lion, the Witch, and the Wardrobe*, and I asked the class to predict what was going to happen in the next chapter, which was titled "Deeper Magic from the Dawn of Time." Arlis raised his hand and said, "I think there is going to be an older spell that is good that is going to cancel out the bad one." He couldn't have been more correct, and, let me tell you, I sure milked that for all it was worth. I pointed out to all the kids how brilliant his prediction was and how proud of him I was for figuring that out. Then I asked a few of my colleagues to do me a favor and mention to Arlis that they had heard he made some really good observations about the novel we were reading. I called his mom and told her I was proud of Arlis for paying attention during reading and that he was doing an excellent job of participating in class. Was I going a little overboard? Well, maybe so, but it sure began to pay off.

When we got to a new chapter and I asked for predictions, Arlis's hand was the first in the air. He wasn't always right, but I acted as if I hadn't really noticed that. No matter how "out there" his answers were, instead of saying he was wrong, I said something like, "Oh, I can see where you're coming from, Arlis, but can someone tell me . . ." I worked very hard to build up his confidence; the last thing I wanted to do was tear it down. Sometimes while we read I said something to this effect, "That was a really difficult passage, and I want to make sure you all understand what the author was really trying to say. I mean, I'm sure Arlis and a few others of you understood it, but I want to make sure we all get the big picture."

By the end of the year, Arlis became one of my best reading students, and he scored a level 4 on his end-of-year reading test. Simply through receiving that praise and building his confidence, he began to believe he was an exceptional reader, and in the process, he became one. Of course, high expectations, individual instruction, and other motivating factors all played into Arlis's success, but I know that the key, without a doubt, was praise.

Sometimes, however, praise is not enough. I usually take

my students on twenty-five to thirty small trips a year, but I don't necessarily take the entire class each time. I usually begin the year by taking small trips with just three or four kids. That is a very manageable number, and we go somewhere that doesn't require a lot of planning or extra effort on my part, like the movies or a museum. It's quick and it's easy, and it has a definite impact on the climate of the class. When the other students find out I took a group to the movies, they wonder why they weren't picked. They want to know what they have to do to get picked. I select the initial group for behaving well or doing good work, so it translates into good motivation for the rest of the class.

Once I arranged to take a group of twelve students to attend a practice of the North Carolina Tar Heels basketball team. For those kids, it was like a dream; they were all thrilled to go. To prepare, they had to use the players' statistics to complete math worksheets and other assignments. They also had to study the history of the university and the basketball program.

A few days before the trip, one of the students, Rodriquez, hadn't learned all of the information and hadn't turned in his worksheets. I told him, in front of the other students, that if he didn't have them the next day he wouldn't be allowed to go. The next day he frantically walked in and claimed he couldn't finish the worksheets because he had left one of them at school. I told him, without blinking an eye, that he couldn't go. I could tell he was destroyed and it was obvious he was trying to hide that from the other students. The entire time we were at the Dean Dome, I thought about Rodriquez and how much that experience would have meant to him. The students were even allowed to shoot around with some of the Tar Heel players. It was a once-in-a-lifetime opportunity and I had denied Rodriquez the chance to go. No, he didn't complete his work, but I never should have said he wouldn't be allowed to go if he didn't turn in those worksheets. In some cases, stipulations like that shouldn't be used. You have to look at the big picture and ask yourself what, in the end, is best for the child. A better punishment for Rodriquez would have been to have him stay after school every day for a week doing extra work. I should have never put his chances of going on the trip in jeopardy. Taking away some things is okay, and of course it's okay to punish kids by denying them privileges, but we should never deny them experiences that may motivate and inspire them or change their lives for the better.

I have one more comment about rewards and punishments—they should be given immediately after the action. Dealing with administration can sometimes make that impossible. In some schools, if a child is written up for a disciplinary action, it may be days before the child is called to the office or disciplined in any way. Sometimes schools name a "Student of the Week." That child receives some reward like free ice cream from the principal, but it could be weeks before it actually happens. Imagine how we would feel if our paycheck (our reward) were two weeks late. What if during a basketball game a referee blew his whistle for a foul that was committed in the previous quarter? It just doesn't make sense.

One time I put the students on teams of seven and told them that I would order a pizza for the group that scored the highest on their Friday spelling test. Well, that week I saw the highest spelling scores of the year, and the winning group ended up scoring all 100s. They were thrilled and were ready for the pizza that day, but I forgot to call in time for the pizza to be delivered for lunch. I told them I would order it on the following Monday, but then two of the kids from the team were absent. Before I knew it, it was Friday again, and they still hadn't gotten their pizza. Needless to say, that Friday I saw some of the lowest test scores of the year.

On the other hand, I had two students get in a fight in the bathroom one morning. Why must they always start the fights in the bathroom? There I go, running in, slipping and sliding, grabbing one boy with one hand and one in the other. They were huffing and puffing and furious, and I took them to the office to see the principal. She said she would deal with them immediately, but as our class walked by on the way to the lunchroom, I noticed the boys still sitting in the office. They said they had not even seen the principal yet, so I just took them with us to eat. After lunch, I talked with both boys and we worked out the problem. That happened on a Wednesday. The following Monday, the in-school suspension teacher arrived and said the boys were to spend two days with her for punishment. By that time, the boys were fine; they were doing their work and they were focused on what was going on in class. The incidents surrounding the fight were far removed from their minds, yet they were now, almost a week later, being punished.

To be effective, discipline and praise must be given immediately. The closer they are given to the occurrence, the more influence they have on the child.

# IN CLOSING...

When I finished writing this book, I was one happy person. Getting so many thoughts, ideas, and stories on paper was much harder than I first anticipated. I thought I was finally done when my best friend, Amanda, asked me, "So, how does your book end? I just hate it when a book doesn't have a good ending." I took a deep breath and gulped. I respect her opinion, and her statement scared me. How am I supposed to end this book? Well, for starters, I know at least Amanda is going to like this ending because her name is in it (Amanda Rae Nixon from Hope Mills, North Carolina), but for everyone else I felt it needed something more. As I tried to decide on an ending, I talked with my co-teacher from Snowden Elementary School, Barbara Jones. She said to me, "So, Mr. Clark, please tell me you wrote in the book what your meaning of life is. I love to hear you talk about it." I hadn't mentioned it up to this point, and it seemed like a fitting ending, so here goes...

To me, life is all about experiences, the ones you make for yourself and the ones you make for others. As a teacher, and as a person, I try to give special moments to people. I mentioned earlier that I once took students to the campus of the University of North Carolina to watch a college basketball practice. When it was over, I told the students, "Kids, I know I told you we were only here to watch, but you all need to go get changed, because we're going to get to play a game in the Dean Dome!" I still remember the look on Kenneth's face as he jumped up and down over and over. The expression in his eyes was pure joy, total elation, and shock. I know that is a moment he will never forget as long as he lives.

Moments like that occurred when I announced to the students they were going to the White House, surprised the students in Harlem with the trip to Los Angeles, had my students in the front rows of *The Phantom of the Opera* on Broadway, and every time I put my students in situations where they felt totally alive and knew they were truly living. Giving them those types of moments, making those types of emotions for others, is, to me, what life is about. If this book does nothing else, I hope it inspires you to make more of a difference in the lives of children. Guide them as they grow, show them in every way possible they are cared for, and make special moments for them that add magic to their lives, motivate them to make a difference in the lives of others, and, most importantly, teach them to be good people.

# ABOUT THE AUTHOR

**Ron Clark** is the *New York Times* bestselling author of *The Essential 55*, which has sold more than one million copies in the U.S. and has been published in twenty-five different languages. He has been named "American Teacher of the Year" by Disney and Oprah Winfrey's first "Phenomenal Man." He founded the Ron Clark Academy in Atlanta, Georgia, which more than 50,000 educators from around the world have visited to learn about the extraordinary ways that teachers and parents of RCA have helped children achieve great success.

@ronclark__

@mrronclark_